The Grand Butterfly Gathering

WINGS OF CHANGE FOR A TRANSFORMED WORLD

An Inspired Curation
By Dr. M Teresa Lawrence

New Life Clarity Publishing
205 West 300 South, Brigham City, Utah 84302
Http://newlifeclarity.com/

The Right of Dr. M Teresa Lawrence to be identified as the Author of the work has been asserted by her in accordance with the Copyright Act 1988.

New Life Clarity Publishing
name has been established by NLCP.
All Rights Reserved.

No part of this publication may be reproduced, distributed, or transmitted in any form or by any means, including photocopying, recording, or other electronic or mechanical methods without the prior and express written permission of the author or publisher, except in the case of brief quotations embodied in critical reviews and certain other noncommercial uses permitted by copyright law.

Printed in the United States of America

ISBN- 979-8-33-024188-0

Copyright@2024 Dr. M Teresa Lawrence

Dedication

To the butterflies, who grace us with their delicate beauty
and remind us of nature's power of transformation.

To the wind that carries them, the rivers that nourish life,
the vast oceans that connect us all and the stars that guide us.

To the natural world all around us, through which
we feel the presence of the divine.

May this book celebrate humanity's deep connection with nature
and serve as a global call for peace, harmony and positive change.

The Grand Butterfly Gathering is a coming together to appreciate
the wonders of the Earth and all its creatures, and to unite our
hopes and prayers for a better tomorrow.

The Grand Butterfly Gathering

A FORWARD BY DR. JUDITH RICH

As her coach and mentor, I have had the honor of witnessing the journey of Dr. M Teresa Lawrence from her early aspirations of invisibility to the manifestation of her vision—The Grand Butterfly Gathering in Jackson, WY on June 29, 2024. It has been an extraordinary experience!

This book, The Grand Butterfly Gathering: Wings of Change for a Transformed World marks a pivotal chapter in her story, a testament to the power of dreams transformed into reality.

When I close my eyes, I can vividly imagine her vision made manifest:

The Grand Butterfly Gathering, a vibrant spectacle with hundreds, perhaps thousands, of individuals dressed as butterflies. They will fill the streets and open spaces of Jackson, WY, a beautiful mountain town, united by Dr. Lawrence's vision of praying for world peace. The peaceful flutter of countless wings will paint a powerful picture of harmony and unity.

This gathering of gentle creatures symbolizes tranquility and hope, elements that are deeply embedded in our collective consciousness.

The transformation from caterpillar to butterfly is not just a natural phenomenon, but also a powerful metaphor for human potential and renewal. It is this story of profound change that captivates us, reminding us of our capacity for growth and rebirth.

Within every caterpillar are imaginal cells, unique to their kind. These cells carry the blueprint of a future butterfly, dormant yet destined to define its fate. Similarly, each human being harbors potential, often unknown until the moment of awakening. This metamorphosis begins inconspicuously within the confines of a cocoon, where the caterpillar dissolves into a seemingly formless goo. Yet, from this dissolution emerges a new form, a beautiful butterfly ready to embrace its destiny, illustrating the potential that lies in periods of transition and seeming chaos.

Our own lives mirror this cycle of transformation. Over the course of fifty years, I have had the privilege of facilitating the transformation of countless individuals, guiding them to uncover and embrace the possibilities within. Dr. James Hillman's concept in The Soul's Code beautifully parallels this idea, suggesting that we are each born with a unique code that shapes our destiny, much like the genetic material that guides the caterpillar.

Dr. Lawrence's vision for The Grand Butterfly Gathering, and the creation of this book, are manifestations of her dedication to this transformative journey. She has curated a collection of writings that not only share her vision but also amplify it, encouraging us to explore and harness our latent potential.

The authors featured in this book offer their unique perspectives, weaving together themes of inspiration, motivation, and the infinite possibilities that arise when we choose to transform ourselves and, by extension, the world around us.

Their collective message is clear: transformation is not just an individual journey but also a communal quest, moving us from a state of fear and scarcity to one of abundance, peace, and love.

This dream of transformation is ancient, woven into the fabric of human history, often viewed as a utopian fantasy. Yet, history itself is punctuated with moments of profound change and realization, reminding us that what seems impossible can become inevitable.

John Lennon captured this essence in his song "Imagine," a melody that has become a timeless anthem for peace and unity. It invites us to dream together, to believe in a unified world. This book, like the song, is a call to action—a call to dream, to dare, and to do.

As you delve into the pages of this book, you are invited to embark on your own journey of transformation. May the stories and insights within inspire you to discover your own imaginal cells—those aspects of your being that contain the blueprint of who you might become.

Let this book be a catalyst, a guide, and a companion as you navigate the path of your own evolution.

Through the metaphor of the butterfly, we are reminded of our resilience and our capacity to emerge from periods of darkness into light. Each chapter in this book serves as a reminder that every end is a new beginning, every challenge is an opportunity for growth, and every individual has the potential to contribute to a more peaceful, joyful, and loving world.

In closing, my heartfelt congratulations to Dr. Lawrence and each of the authors represented in this book. Their courage to dream and to manifest those dreams into reality is a beacon of hope for all of us. May their dedication inspire you to catch the fire of transformation, to dare to dream the dreams you have yet to dream, and to step boldly into the journey of your own transformation.

May the unfolding of your own story remind you that no matter the circumstances of your beginnings, the potential for greatness lies within you. Like the butterfly, you are destined to soar, to explore, and to thrive. Trust in yourself, embrace your journey, and remember: in every moment, anything is possible.

Introduction

Dr. M Teresa Lawrence

How to Give a Movement Wings Transformation is the essence of life itself. We are all on a never-ending journey of growth, evolution, and becoming. Sometimes the process is messy, emotional, and heart wrenching, but it is a vital part of our human experience. We must embrace the challenges and difficulties along the way, for they are what shape us, refine us, and ultimately propel us towards our highest selves. It is okay to cry, to feel the depths of our emotions as they pass through our bodies like waves upon the shore. In those moments of vulnerability and rawness, we must ask ourselves, "What am I meant to learn from this? How can I use this

Introduction

experience as a catalyst for bringing more love and light into my life and the world around me?" We are all storytellers, weaving the intricate tapestries of our lives with every thought, word, and action. These individual threads intertwine, forming a communal narrative that ultimately shapes our global story. It is a profound responsibility, yet also a tremendous gift, for we have the power to choose the tales we tell and the realities we create. When did we allow the darkness of hatred, prejudice, and exploitation to become woven into the fabric of our shared story? When did we lose sight of our shared humanity and the inherent dignity and worth of every soul? The pull towards negativity and division is ever-present, but we must resist it with every fiber of our being. I am a dreamer, a visionary who dares to imagine the seemingly impossible. In addition, when I share these dreams, I am often met with laughter, doubt, and dismissal. "It cannot be done!" they say. "You have no experience. What makes you think you can do it?" To which I reply, "I know I can do it because I believe I can." It is the power of belief and thought that guides my path. I have an unwavering faith in the Divine, and I know that the Divine has an unwavering belief in me. I believe that we are here on this earth to uplift one another, to be beacons of light in the darkness, and to help each other soar to ever-greater heights. Life can feel messy, confrontational, and harsh at times, but it is through those challenges that we learn and grow. Look back on your own journey and reflect on the lessons you learned as you walked through the darkness, with only your faith as a guide. Trust in the power of grace and spirit that surrounds us. It guides us, keeps us safe, and opens doors when we are truly ready to step through them. Life itself is the greatest gift we have been given, and each day is an opportunity to embrace it fully. I give thanks daily for the privilege of meeting new people, facing new challenges, and actively creating a world that I love. I know that I am the author of my own reality, and as such, I intentionally weave light into each day by asking, "Who can I bless today? Whose life can I touch and uplift?" The COVID years stripped me, and this world, of so many loved ones – my mother, my godmother, my mentor, and countless dear friends. It was a harsh wake-up call, reminding me to live each day with intention and clarity, pursuing my dreams with every breath, for tomorrow is never promised. I choose to engage fully with the world, to get messy, to share my dreams boldly, and to breathe them into reality through my thoughts, prayers, and actions. If you are reading this and have a list of dreams that you have never pursued, for a myriad of reasons, I implore you: take out that list and choose one dream to focus on. The day I decided to bring my dreams into reality, my life was forever transformed. I do not even recognize the person I was before, living in a world of lack, sacrifice, and control – a martyr, a savior, a people-pleaser who sacrificed truth to avoid hurting feelings. It took a pandemic and the loss of those I loved most to wake me up to the power and freedom of walking in truth and integrity. When you live in alignment with your deepest truths, you are never lost. A profound peace permeates your mind, body, and life – a state of nirvana that is yours to savor. The past holds no power, for you realize that it is no longer happening, and dwelling on it only gives energy to stories that no longer concern you. In this state of being, you realize that you are the master of your destiny. Your mind, through the power of storytelling, desire, and intentional action, holds the key to your success. Faith is an essential part of the journey, the path your mind follows to unlock the doors that lead to your dreams. The Trueness Project is my dream and it is designed to help others live in authenticity so that they may realize their dreams. So when the Divine whispers in your ear and offers you a gift, listen. You may not always enjoy where you are being led, but you will emerge from each challenge wiser and more prepared to handle the next wondrous, magical opportunity that awaits. For me, that opportunity is The Grand Butterfly Gathering on June 29, 2024. The joy of orchestrating a worldwide community building

Introduction

event with the intention of uplifting the planet as we play as children dressed as butterflies is truly magical. Thinking about it simply makes me smile and makes my heart truly flutter. You may be blessed, as I have, to meet fellow dreamers, visionaries, and "weavers of light" who value your dreams, honor your journey, and weave their own light into your story. These souls are true blessings, and I am grateful for every gift and lesson I have received through the years from those who have shared my dreams and their radiance. The authors in this book are weavers of light. They have blessed me, and I have blessed them in return. This is the beauty and power of language and the written word – words have the ability to breathe dreams into reality. The story you weave into this world determines the outcome of your life. When you meet someone who shares your dreams and believes in their inevitability, watch as magic unfolds before your eyes. The authors in this book all believe in the transformative power of life itself. They have endured great hardships, but instead of being consumed by them, they have used those experiences as mirrors for self-reflection and catalysts for profound personal transformation. Their chapters reflect their struggles and their shifts in consciousness, a testament to the resilience of the human spirit and our infinite capacity for growth and rebirth. Together, several of us traveled to Costa Rica in February 2024 to set the intention for our June 29th event, aimed at spreading peace and love across the planet. Seven strangers came together, and through play, vulnerability, and the sharing of our stories and dreams, we became more than friends – we became a mastermind, united in our vision and purpose. In complete trust and shared communion, we prayed and celebrated the profound connection between humanity and the natural world. Just as the butterfly emerges from its chrysalis, transformed and taking flight on newly formed wings, so too can a singular moment of unified thought and intention become something transcendent, a MOVEMENT that takes flight and soars. On June 29th in Jackson, Wyoming, a movement takes Flight– a moment where people from all walks of life unite with a shared vision of peace, harmony, creativity, community, and love blossoming all around us. It is a moment that reminds the world that despite our diversity, we are one human family, interwoven with the wondrous tapestry of nature itself. Let our unified hearts become a powerful prayer, a collective intention for peace, rebirth, and the uplifting of all life on this sacred planet we call home. This is how we give a movement wings – by pooling our dreams, our beliefs, our hopes, and our love into a singular, powerful force for positive change. Join us on this journey. Become a weaver of light, sharing your dreams, your stories, your truths, and your vision for a more beautiful world. Together, we can transform reality and uplift humanity to new heights of compassion, understanding, and enlightenment. The Trueness Project welcomes all weavers of the light! The time is now. The path has been prepared. Let us step forward together, hand in hand, heart to heart, and give this great Movement the wings it needs to soar. The Grand Butterfly Gathering: Wings of Change for a Transformed World is the calling card. It is the whisper. The Trueness Project has shared the dream. Weave your light into our dream and together let's give our worldwide MOVEMENT wings!

About The Curator

Dr. M Teresa Lawrence, the visionary Curator of the Grand Butterfly Movement and the President and Executive Director of the Trueness Project, has dedicated her life to the pursuit of truth and the uplifting of others through the power of storytelling.

With an unwavering belief that "Truth is the path to PEACE", Teresa has embarked on a mission to uplift the vibration of the planet through transformative experiences and the power of unity.

Driven by a profound vision of an open path filled with infinite love and blessed by nature, Teresa sought to create an event that would bring the world together in a shared moment of reflection and prayer. On June 29, 2024, she organized a world record-breaking event, inviting participants from every corner of the globe to unite in a collective prayer for peace. Teresa firmly believes that "Prayer lights our path as we seek truth" and through this global initiative, she aimed to ignite a spark of hope and compassion in the hearts of people everywhere.

While prayer may start the journey, Teresa recognized and has always believed that the key to building a true sense of community lies in the joy of playing as children, without the filters and barriers that often separate us as adults. By encouraging individuals to embrace their inner child and engage in moments of pure, unadulterated joy, Teresa believes that we can break down the walls that divide us and foster a deep sense of connection and understanding.

In her tireless pursuit of truth and peace, Teresa's nonprofit, the Trueness Project declared June 29th, 2024 as the first International Day of Trueness. This special day serves as an invitation for people worldwide to take a step back from the chaos of daily life and embark on a journey of introspection and self-discovery. By reflecting inwardly and connecting with what is truly authentic and genuine within ourselves, Teresa believes that we can lay the foundation for a more peaceful and harmonious world.

At the core of Teresa's philosophy is the belief that the path to peace begins with truth. Through the Trueness Project, she has created a platform for individuals to explore their own truths, share their stories, and connect with others on a profound level. By fostering an environment of openness, honesty, and vulnerability, Teresa aims to create a ripple effect of positive change that will extend far beyond the boundaries of any single event or initiative.

Dr. M Teresa Lawrence's unwavering commitment to truth and peace serves as a beacon of hope in a world that often seems plagued by conflict and division. Through her visionary leadership, innovative projects, and boundless compassion, she continues to inspire and empower individuals across the globe to embrace their authentic selves and work towards a brighter, more peaceful future for all.

Content

Dominic Obadiah 1
  ○ Why Service to Humanity 1
Sabrina Castellanos 10
  ○ Discovering the Magic of Transformation -
    Reconnecting with My Inner Being 10
George Yang 16
  ○ Navigating Life's Challenges: A Tale of Perseverance,
    Hope, and Empowerment 16
Muriel Blanc 22
  ○ Teenage Healer: One Girl's Journey to Save Her Mom 22
Ken D. Foster 31
  ○ The World Upshift Movement: Unraveling the Butterfly Effect 31
Paul Dangal 42
  ○ Chain Break 42
Emmanuel Sananka 49
  ○ Wings of Change: Empowering the Maasai Community
    through Education, Mentorship, and Advocacy 49
Shauna Sommer 55
  ○ Breaking Barriers with Broken Wings 55
Jonathan Brierre 62
  ○ Moving From Force to Flow - A Journey for Truth,
    Transformation, and Surrender 62
Benvictor Makau Isaac 70
  ○ Soaring Through Transformation, a Flap at a Time 70

Edinah Kangwana 78
- The Gift of Personal Transformation 78

Janice Burt 89
- One Fear per Year 89

Chris Murillo 97
- The Quest for Perfection 97

Obed Charles 100
- The Blessed Touch 100

Pattie Godfrey-Sadler 105
- The Meraki of YOU 105

Dominic Obadiah

WHY SERVICE TO HUMANITY

INTRODUCTION

Service to humanity is as old as the universe itself. Humanity has ever since helped those that needed food, shelter and clothing. All religious believes have traces of serving humanity.

Service can come in form of tangible commodity or even an act of kindness. It involves sharing ones time and resource to someone else who is in need.

This generous act brings hope and helps those helped to keep pressing towards the mark thus inspiring them towards their own success.

Service to humanity makes the world a better place as it raises vibrational energy of love in the entire universe.

Here are some of the benefits of serving humanity:

i. Brings hope to the hopeless.
ii. Helps improve self-esteem of those helped.
iii. Promotes love in the universe.
iv. Helps ignite purpose.
v. Rekindles a good feeling to those helped.

Swami Vivekananda an Indian monk once said, *"Service to humanity is service to God."* This saying is true because serving humanity is a higher calling than self. Abundance of resources does not qualify one to be a giver. I have seen the rich of richest being so mean. Some even die with billions of dollars in their bank accounts. Their immediate neighbors starve to death but the rich mean at heart never blinks.

This brings me to the question that I always ask my audience, "What is your true purpose and calling?"

SERVICE TO HUMANITY IS A CALLING

This is the inner voice that speaks to you when you are resting in the middle of the night. To some this still voice speaks when one is in line with nature and in highest consciousness. Again, to some it may come as a dream or a vision that is very clear. This voice comes with, the What, When, Why and How. The "Who" is sometimes not clear until at a later stage.

Service to humanity is not a career neither is it a part time or full time job. It is a feeling or an urge to serve others.

This feeling does not have an expiry date. Some serve until their last breath. Others can choose to serve to a certain time.

As for me, I received my true purpose and calling to serve humanity a decade ago. I was working at that time. Then an opportunity presented itself to guide a visiting group from U.S that was doing a ten-day community service in western Kenya. Since I am a trained tour guide, I got the opportunity to help guide this group for the entire days they were in the country. I remember it was the seventh day when we visited an orphanage. This children's home had abandoned children aged between one and eight years. I had never been to a children's home. There was this little baby whose name I learnt later was called Angel. She was about 2 years of age. I carried her in my arms and she stared at me as if we bonded. She got hold of my thumb and refused to let go! Time came when everybody was leaving the home but Angel refused to let me go. She was forcefully taken away from me. For the first time in my life, I became emotional and I shed tears.

In Africa, crying has all long been viewed as a sign of weakness. Men are trained not to show this weakness. This day I realized shedding tears as man was okay. It did not make me weak but rather exposed the inner self and revealed to me whom I was created to be and what my true purpose was.

I am called to serve humanity. Since that day, I felt so good and started a journey to touch lives and make the world a better place than I found it. Each time I serve, I feel so good. I feel fulfilled and want to do more and more.

Mother Teresa is remembered in history for dedicating her entire life to serve and work with the poor. Her love for the poor is well documented from Calcutta to all corners of the world. She showered love, hope and sense of purpose for thousands of people both young and old.

In our country, thousands of individuals have become philanthropists. These are people who either as an individual or as a group work towards helping the needy amongst communities.

Philanthropists have formed organizations, which are community based, country based or even international organizations. These organizations raise money in form of charity or from existing humanitarian bodies and use it to address famine, flood, shelter, clothing, education, conflict and disease outbreak amongst communities that are suffering. Organizations such as the international commission of Red Cross, the Red Crescent Society, the order of Malta among others address a wide range of needs among them treating the wounded in a conflict zone, evacuation of non-combat to safety and providing basic needs among others.

In the current century, service to humanity has evolved to include humanitarian diplomacy, humanitarian chaplaincy and humanitarian negotiations. Executive training is needed in order to know how to advocate for the vulnerable. Some conflicts are inter-nations thus calling for professional negotiation and mediation. Humanitarian negotiators and diplomats engage policy makers and opinion leaders at all times as they advocate for the vulnerable in the society. They help soldiers in the field, governments, international organizations and local organizations to understand how to do humanitarian work effectively and upholding the fundamental principles of humanity, neutrality, impartiality and independence.

United Nations under the office of coordination of humanitarian affairs (UNOCHA) plays a key role in the humanitarian space by receiving relief fund and dispatching it to organizations that qualify. Some organizations that apply and qualify for funding from UNOCHA collaborate and partner with local organizations and other humanitarian actors in giving out humanitarian aid to the vulnerable people affected either by natural or manufactured calamities. These calamities include; conflicts, famine, earthquakes, floods and disease outbreak. Humanitarian work has become so complex but simple if we get the right tools and engage the right humanitarian actors. The key phrase here is, *'Service to humanity and providing solutions to those hurting.'*

MY JOURNEY AS A HUMANITARIAN

My humanitarian journey started a decade ago. I was working in the tourism industry when I connected with a woman called Ann Webb. She told me she was a life coach. I had never heard anything about life coaching. In fact, I thought she was a soccer coach in that matter. She however made it clear to me what she was doing in life and what life coaching meant. She told me that she helped her clients set crystal clear goals in all the six areas of their lives. Her program was unique in the sense that it helped one to set goals, pursue their purpose in life and stay accountable to their set goals by working daily towards achieving them. I took Ann's program online and later got certified as a life coach. I became the first certified life coach in Africa under Ideal Life Vision.

Fast forward, I discovered my true purpose and calling as I helped my friends and my community to create goals for themselves. I believe I got reborn. Each time I helped others set their goals and work towards them, I felt fulfilled, certified and happy. Ann was thrilled by the results I was getting just in a short time. The things I had committed in my ideal life vision started happening. Was it magic? No. It was getting crystal clear on what I wanted. There is power when you write your visions down. It is more powerful when you engage your sub conscious mind towards a specific goal. You will only settle once you achieve your results. I loved this program because it was simple and duplicable. The first step was to know what you want then proceed towards creating goals around what you want to achieve. The written goals can be recorded in a phone with classical music in the background. The classical music helps activate ones subconscious mind and the message. Our mind works best when it is active. The final part is to commit to listen to your recorded life vision daily. This will help wake you up from your comfort zone and push you off the limits to work towards doing the things you have written down and recorded. There is a quote in the holy book that says, '*As a man thinketh and believeth in his heart so he is.*' It has proven that wherever you divert your energies to, you will get results. Sadly, we use most of our time on negative vibrational energy. How about working positively towards what we want! We will achieve a lot more and make the world a better place for everyone.

Over a decade, I have served as a humanitarian and a leader in various capacities. My pure love for humanity saw me resign from my active employment in the tourism industry to follow my heart desire. To me this is a higher calling to serve than a career. Over the years I have worked with different organizations among them; Global life vision, Family humanitarian, Humans of peace education, iChangenations (ICN) among others.

I am currently the Kenyan president for **The Trueness Project** a 501c organization that has its headquarter in Jackson Hole Wyoming, USA. Dr. M Teresa Lawrence is the founding president. The organization helps bright but needy students in Kenya access scholarship to study. Besides the organization does mentorship to college and high school students and helps end period shame by providing sanitary towels to teenage girls.

Green energy is also part of The Trueness Project- agenda as the organization seeks funds to provide solar to rural homes to help rural children study and do their homework.

My role as TTP Kenyan president is to work with schools and identify needy but bright students and forward their details to the organization for consideration. Once approved I facilitate school fee payment and link the sponsored students to individual sponsors. I also make sure that academic reports are sent to the sponsors each academic term / semester. I encourage students to write letters to their sponsors in order to create a relationship beyond tuition aid. This responsibility gives me inner joy as lives are changed, transformed and empowered.

I am a believer of sustainable humanitarian aid instead of hand-out donations. Sponsoring students, helps transform them to future leaders who will then carry it forward and transform their families, communities, their country and the entire global family.

My humanitarian journey has affected over twenty thousand students mostly in high schools and colleges across Africa. I have mentored students in Ghana, DRC Congo, Uganda, Tanzania and Kenya. Many have received and used my career goal setting-coaching program to help them achieve higher results and become responsible citizens. Others have received tuition sponsorships from various organizations I have worked with in the past and present. One of the schools that has benefited heavily is Manga Girls in Nyamira County. Over a hundred students have received school fees for a whole year, water tanks have been donated, books among other aid. I have personally adopted over twenty children and paid their school fees.

Eunice's family comprises of six girls whose parents died four years ago leaving them as orphans. I took them in and took Joyce to a boarding school and put Asnath and Eunice to a day school. I helped them access solar and water tank from a friend.

Valeria comes from Kisii, Kenya. She is 13 years old. She is the first-born girl in a family of three girls. Their mother is a mental health case. She left home and has never been traced. I decided to adopt these three beautiful girls who now live with their grandparents. Each year I raise money on my birthday and use it to pay school fees, buy clothes, books, and shoes just to cushion them. I am happy to have helped them build a house they can shelter in. They live in, Kisii, Kenya

Naomi is one of my success story. She dropped out of school due to lack of school fees. She unfortunately conceived. I re-enrolled her back to high school and she did so well in her national exams. She is set to join university this year and train as a high school teacher. The good news is you can adopt a school or even a student by paying school fees.

I would love to talk about Marion, a young girl whose parents were murdered in cold blood six years ago. Criminals broke into their home at night and shot dead their parents, burnt them with an acid. The acid also affected Marion since she was in the room as well. She was thirteen years by that time.

I was introduced to Marion's family five years ago and I decided to help educate Marion. Through friends, I was able to see Marion finish high school. This year she has joined college to study bachelor of nursing. I am so happy I ended up becoming her adopted brother. Her bother won a green card and moved to the U.S for work.

Women have not been left out in my endeavors. I have helped so many of them with sustainable development projects. These projects include vegetable gardens, goats, chicken and cows. Some have been helped to obtain skills on tailoring and dressmaking, hair salon services, and sewing among others. Through these skills, some have started small-scale businesses and are now getting income to support their families. Over six communities in Kenya, Tanzania and Uganda have received donations of protecting natural spring water. Through the help of a village drill machine, we have been able to sink a borehole for the Nyamuya village in Gusii land, Kisii-Kenya.

Elementary schools across East Africa have benefited with sports gear mostly soccer / net balls, school repairs, painting of schools, pens and books among others donations. Like a butterfly that transforms itself, we believe in education as a tool to help students in the transformational journey as they work towards becoming great leaders of tomorrow. It is empowering a student at a time.

Besides schools, I was able to help over 200 families with special needs during covid-19. I decided to show them love by providing them with food and clothing. These small acts of kindness create positive vibrational energy thus increasing love amongst the underprivileged. I am a strong believer of the universal laws. I study the law of attraction and I love the results I am creating.

Due to my dedication and commitment to serve humanity, I have travelled to the Netherlands, Turkey, Costa Rica, Germany, Ghana, Rwanda, Tanzania to attend both humanitarian and leadership conferences. I have used the knowledge I learn to improve on my services both at home and abroad.

Because of my dedication to serve humanity, I have been honored locally and internationally. I am a world civility ambassador under iChangenations (ICN-U.S.A), Presidential Honor Recipient (HSC), National Hero (Kenya), Peace Ambassador among others.

The honors and recognition withstanding, I love serving humanity.

I am a father of two and a loving husband to my beautiful wife called Rose.

What we want to see happen to us we must do to others. We reap what we sow. Together lets help promote humanitarian activities from wherever we are. I invite you to join us be and be part of the Trueness Project by visiting our website www.yourtrueness.org lets create pure life. "Pura vida"

Sabrina Castellanos

DISCOVERING THE MAGIC OF TRANSFORMATION - RECONNECTING WITH MY INNER BEING

Let me tell you why. In February 2024, my life took an unexpected turn. I checked my bank account and faced a bleak reality: I had a million-dollar debt and a negative balance. The red numbers froze my heart, and anxiety seized my mind. I felt fear, desperation, and sadness like never before. I found myself at the bottom of both financial and emotional abyss, something I had never experienced in my 40s. I had closed one of my businesses two months earlier after trying a thousand ways to keep it afloat, but we could not do it anymore and the best decision was to close it. By that time, I had been dragging a debt for months. The income was not enough to cover all expenses, and little by little, month by month, the savings dwindled until the day the account went into the red. It was a dark and fearful day. I did not know what to do; my heart and mind were pounding with anxiety, seeking alternatives to move forward. It was in this moment of darkness that I decided to use all the tools at my disposal: leadership techniques, spirituality, and above all, gratitude. Gratitude became my compass, guiding me toward the light in the midst of the storm. I learned to look beyond scarcity and find abundance in the small blessings of life. On one hand, a company was closing, but on the other hand, a company was growing and doors were opening. My passion for helping grew as much as the number of people I assisted through my consultations and coaching. However, debts kept piling up based on years of expenses higher than the income I received. Nevertheless, the path to transformation was not easy. I faced internal conflicts, and fought against guilt and frustration. However, each internal battle brought me one-step closer to the radical acceptance of my worth. Everyday life reminded me why that episode happened to me, for my growth and learning. I remember one particular day, coming home, I saw my cousin talking to my parents. We started talking about abundance and he said to me, "Money doesn't define me, if I run out of money today; it doesn't define who I am." At that moment, my ego short-circuited, until I finally understood after asking myself: who am I? My cousin reminded me that money does not define my value. It was a divine message that resonated deep within me, changing my perspective and empowering me to take control of my life. It was that divine message that came to me through my cousin. That same week I received an invitation to a gratitude course, a course that has changed my life, generating peace within me and recognizing that I am abundant. I exchanged fear for peace and love. Creating a mindset shift and reprogramming myself, using gratitude as a technique to raise my vibration.

Other unexpected opportunities began to come into my life, and my vision of the future began to change. I learned to vibrate in the frequency of gratitude and abundance, attracting resources in unexpected ways. Magic began to manifest in my life, reminding me that I am enough and deserving of the best. The turning point and change came with an invitation to a retreat in Costa Rica, thanks to Dr. M Teresa Lawrence of The Trueness Project. I remember being in my room when a text message from Teresa arrived, at that moment I was talking to God asking for a sign that everything would be fine, and then a message from Teresa arrived, the message said: "You are invited to the retreat; I want you to be here with us." In that second, I started to cry because a few days earlier I had been looking at the retreat and had said, "I know that energy would be good for me." I cried knowing that I had manifested that message and it was a divine message that resources come in different ways when one trusts. At that moment, I did not know how I would get the money for the ticket, but I knew I would go. I followed my intuition and destiny took care of it. A few weeks later, I was on my way to Costa Rica. I followed my intuition and trusted, I had no agenda or expectation. It was a journey where I immersed myself in a week of self-discovery and spiritual connection. I got on the plane trusting in Teresa's wonderful energy and something that had been calling me to that country for years. Upon arriving in Costa Rica, a path of trust and surrender began. I remember arriving at night, I was alone, the rest of the group had already arrived, and there was my first test of surrender, upon arrival it was already dark and they were waiting for me, where I trusted the driver who told me that the hotel was an hour and a half from the airport, I got into a van and we left, my fears of having lived in Venezuela tried to come up. There I trusted and surrendered to the wonder and magic that was creating every minute. Upon arriving at the hotel, I realized the great change I had made. I had created being there; thanks to following my intuition I had created being with wonderful and luminous people, as the days passed, I realized that each person in the group reflected an area of me. They were wonderful mirrors that reminded me who I was, who I am. Day by day I was connecting, starting with nature absorbing its wisdom and energy, reconnecting with all the elements. Every day was magical, reconnecting with myself, trusting that I am deserving and the creator of everything I saw, felt, and experienced, I reconnected with love, joy, and fun. On the first day, I met everyone and felt an immediate connection, that same day very early we went on an excursion, they picked us up in a van and we went to a park where they had prepared a full day of excursions, we started with zip-lining in the middle of the jungle, which allowed me to clear any trace of resistance that I felt up to that moment. It made me let go and release any limitation and stress, embracing trees, filling myself with energy, and feeling how my inner child returned to me. The connection with nature made me connect with my Source of creation. It was an experience as if nature and the strength of Costa Rica had called me there to receive a message. After zip-lining, we connected with horses riding wonderful beings while soaking up the sun's energy, feeling and finding inner peace. A wonderful day that invited us to connect with all our senses. To end the day, we went tubing on the rapids, a several-hour experience where I connected on another level with Mother Nature, surrendering, understanding what it is to accept, let go, believe, and trust. I understood that resistance does not lengthen the path. When we accept, create, and trust, the path is easier. I learned that life is like rapids, sometimes it has difficult and tumultuous moments, but if you trust and let yourself go, those moments are necessary to move forward and continue. After a rapid comes calm, and you have to live it, experience it, and enjoy it. The calm in the river must be lived because the current always takes you forward, you can be stuck, but the current always takes you out and moves you forward. Eventually, after a combination of calm and rapids, you reach the bottom and enjoy the satisfaction of reaching the goal. Wow, a first day full of learning, by the end of the afternoon, we felt the connection between us as if we had known each other all our lives. Another powerful moment of the trip was going to the beach, a pristine beach where we walked, dreamed, and felt the energy of the earth and the sea. I screamed like a child and played with the waves, reconnecting with the child that I am and the power of play. We culminated the trip with a connection to the moon and the universe, through a wonderful ceremony where we let go of limiting beliefs and programs and created from love and abundance. The energy was so high that it felt like a dense energy layer; we connected with the fire and saw its power, recognizing that we were as strong as it was. Costa Rica was a journey inward, where I rediscovered my power of creation, my connection with the divine, and my innate happiness. I reconnected with my essence, with my inner child, and with the true magic of life, understanding that I am magic and everything is a change of perception. When there is a change of perception, magic is created and when I create magic, there is manifestation. My intuition became my most faithful guide during this period of transformation. I learned to trust my instincts and the universe's signs, knowing that they always led me toward my higher path. Authenticity and honesty became my allies, remembering that living happily is a choice, a choice that is in my hands. Today, I look back and see the journey I have traveled. I am grateful for every challenge, for every lesson, and for every blessing along the way. If anyone else is facing similar challenges, I want to tell them this: you are never alone. Seek help, keep a clear vision, and hold onto your authenticity. Because if it is for you, it depends on you. Be proud of who you are and always remember to stand in responsibility, not in victimhood. Life is full of magic waiting to be discovered. Open your heart, follow your intuition, and get ready to be amazed by what the universe has in store for you. This is just the beginning of your own transformation story. Let the journey to the best version of yourself begin!

BIOGRAPHY

Sabrina Castellanos is a personal success coach and consultant, specializing in organization, strategic planning, and the creation and implementation of processes for leaders and entrepreneurs. As a coach and consultant, she enhances the development of her clients and community, supporting them in strengthening their leadership, organizing their lives, and strategically planning their ventures. In addition to her role as a coach and consultant, Sabrina is an architect by profession, with over 15 years of experience in project management, process creation, strategic planning, and personnel and management training in Toronto. Currently, Sabrina is the CEO of Two Get There Connections and Co-founder of 2 Be Extraordinary, where she leads initiatives for the development and empowerment of leaders. Her vision is to empower, train, and guide these leaders to transform the world, achieve success, and leave a lasting legacy. She seeks to create an environment where transformation, freedom, and abundance are accessible to every leader, providing the tools and support necessary for them to achieve their full potential and be free to decide when and how they use their time.

George Yang

NAVIGATING LIFE'S CHALLENGES: A TALE OF PERSEVERANCE, HOPE, AND EMPOWERMENT

My journey began in a small town in northeastern China, where the air was crisp, and the streets buzzed with the laughter of children playing. I was born in the year of the tiger, a symbol of strength and resilience, but little did I know the challenges that awaited me. At the tender age of nine, my world turned dark as my eyesight began to fade, casting a shadow over my once vibrant life.

In a time when access to healthcare was scarce, my family embarked on a journey filled with uncertainty and fear. My mother, with only a fifth-grade education, became my unwavering champion. She sought every remedy imaginable, from traditional herbs to acupuncture, in a desperate attempt to restore my sight. Despite the pain and frustration, her love never wavered, and her determination fueled my own resilience.

Two years later, we found ourselves at Tongren Hospital in Beijing, a beacon of hope in our quest for answers. There, a compassionate ophthalmologist delivered the devastating diagnosis of juvenile macular degeneration. Though there was no cure, his honesty and kindness ignited a spark within me, fueling a dream to become a healer like him.

But the path to realizing my dreams was riddled with obstacles. In a society where accommodations for disabled children were virtually non-existent, gaining access to education proved to be a Herculean task. Denied entry into public schools, my mother fought tooth and nail to secure my place in a school that welcomed disabled students. Despite facing skepticism and resistance, I persevered, emerging as the top student in my class.

The lack of accommodations meant that I had to rely on sheer determination and resourcefulness to excel academically. I learned to adapt to my environment, finding creative ways to access course materials, participate in class discussions, and complete assignments. Even after gaining admission to college, the challenges persisted. In China, the college entrance examination, known as the Gaokao, posed an additional hurdle for students with disabilities. Passing the physical examination required for eligibility seemed like an insurmountable barrier. Fortunately, through the advocacy efforts of individuals like Pufang Deng, progress was made in expanding access to education for disabled students. Thanks to his efforts, I secured a place in the only college in China that accepted disabled students, albeit with limited accommodations. Studying Traditional Chinese Medicine provided me with valuable insights and skills, but it also underscored the need for greater inclusivity and accessibility in education. Despite the challenges I faced,

I remained determined to pursue my dream of becoming a doctor, inspired by the compassionate care I received from healthcare professionals.

After college, I found fulfillment working in the rehabilitation department of a public hospital. Each day presented new challenges and opportunities to make a difference in the lives of others. Working alongside a dedicated team of healthcare professionals, I witnessed the transformative power of rehabilitation in helping patients regain their strength, mobility, and independence.

One of the most rewarding aspects of my work was helping stroke patients on their journey to recovery. Through intensive rehabilitation and personalized care, I had the privilege of witnessing their progress and resilience firsthand. Each small victory was a cause for celebration, reaffirming my belief in the resilience of the human spirit.

I still remember the first stroke patient I encountered—a woman in her sixties who had lost all hope after being left unable to care for herself. She expressed feelings of despair and contemplated suicide, believing herself to be a burden on her family. It was a heartbreaking moment, but it fueled my determination to make a difference.

Through intensive rehabilitation and personalized care, we were able to help this patient gradually regain her independence. I worked closely with her, providing encouragement, support, and practical assistance as she relearned essential skills like walking, dressing, and cooking. It was a long and challenging journey, but seeing her smile and hearing her express gratitude made every effort worthwhile.

Over time, I encountered many more patients with similar stories of resilience and perseverance. Each one presented unique challenges, but with teamwork and collaboration, we were able to achieve remarkable outcomes. Whether it was helping a stroke survivor regain the ability to feed themselves or assisting a patient with spinal cord injury in learning to navigate a wheelchair, every small victory was a cause for celebration.

Despite facing repeated rejections from medical schools in China, I refused to give up on my dreams. With the assistance of a friend Terisa, I explored other avenues, eventually finding an opportunity to study chiropractic in the United States. Though daunting, I embraced the challenge, determined to seize this opportunity for a better future.

The transition to life in the US was fraught with challenges, from language barriers to cultural differences. However, through grit and determination, I graduated as the salutatorian of my class.

After completing my studies at Life Chiropractic College West, I set my sights on pursuing further education in medicine. This decision was not made lightly, as it meant delving into a new field and facing a fresh set of challenges. However, with the unwavering support of my family, including my wife Vivian and our two boys, I felt emboldened to take on this new chapter of my journey.

The decision to pursue a career in medicine was met with mixed emotions from my loved ones. On one hand, they were proud of my ambition and determination to further my education. On the other hand, they expressed concerns about the rigorous nature of medical school and the toll it might take on our family life.

Despite these concerns, my family stood by me every step of the way, offering their unconditional love and support. Vivian, in particular, was my rock during this challenging period. As a mother and a wife, she juggled countless responsibilities, ensuring that our home ran smoothly while I focused on my studies.

Her unwavering belief in me never wavered, even when doubts crept into my mind. Whenever I felt overwhelmed or discouraged, she was there to lift my spirits and remind me of my potential. Her boundless optimism and faith in our future gave me the strength to persevere, even in the face of adversity.

Our two boys, though young at the time, also played a crucial role in keeping me motivated and focused. Their laughter and playful antics provided a much-needed respite from the rigors of medical school, reminding me of the joy and beauty of life outside the classroom.

As I immersed myself in my studies, my family became my anchor, grounding me in love and support. They cheered me on through late-night study sessions, celebrated my successes, and offered a shoulder to lean on during moments of doubt and uncertainty.

Their sacrifices did not go unnoticed, and I was determined to make them proud. With their love and encouragement fueling my determination, I poured my heart and soul into my studies, determined to excel and prove that their faith in me was not misplaced.

When the time came to sit for the medical licensing exams, I was filled with a mix of nerves and excitement. The stakes were high, but I knew that I had prepared to the best of my ability, thanks in large part to the unwavering support of my family.

When the results came in, I was elated to learn that I had passed with flying colors. It was a moment of triumph and validation, not just for me, but for my entire family. Their unwavering belief in me had been rewarded, and I was one step closer to realizing my dream of becoming a doctor.

Today, as I prepare to embark on the next chapter of my journey as a resident physician, I am filled with gratitude for the love and support of my family. Their unwavering faith in me has been the driving force behind my success, and I am forever grateful for their presence in my life. With their love as my guiding light, I am ready to embrace the challenges and opportunities that lie ahead, confident in my ability to make a meaningful impact in the world of medicine.

Throughout my journey, I remained devoted to sports, finding solace and strength in physical activity. Swimming and goal ball became wellsprings of joy and empowerment, allowing me to participate in various competitions and garner numerous accolades.

In addition to my academic pursuits, I founded Yang &#39 Classroom, an online learning platform for visually impaired practitioners and therapists. Born out of my own struggles and triumphs, Young &#39 Classroom aims to bridge the gap in educational opportunities for visually impaired individuals in China and beyond.

Through a diverse array of online lectures, workshops, and training sessions, Young &#39 Classroom equips students with the tools they need to succeed in their respective fields. Beyond its role as an educational platform, it serves as a community and support network for visually impaired individuals, fostering a spirit of collaboration and mutual support.

As I reflect on my journey, I am filled with gratitude for the unwavering support of my family, friends, and mentors who have helped me surmount countless obstacles. From the trials of my childhood to the triumphs of my adulthood, each challenge has molded me into the individual I am today. With courage, resilience, and an unswerving commitment to making a difference, I am poised to embrace the opportunities and challenges that lie ahead, confident in my ability to inspire change and empower others to realize their full potential.

Muriel Blanc

TEENAGE HEALER: ONE GIRL'S JOURNEY TO SAVE HER MOM

At sixteen, most teenagers are focused on things like getting their driver's license, trying to look cool in front of their crush, and desperately hoping they don't get another pimple before prom. But not Muriel. This feisty, bespectacled lass had bigger issues on her mind—like singlehandedly saving her mother's life through the power of positive thinking and some healing techniques passed down through the ages.

It all started when Muriel's mom, Jackie, suddenly fell walking in the street and could not even lift a pencil even though she was an athlete and super active. The doctors delivered a devastating diagnosis that would shake any family to its core. Autoimmune disease and severe MS? In layman's terms, that's the doctor's code for "Say goodbye to walking, running, lifting anything, and enjoying life." The prognosis was about as uplifting as an IV drip of straight lemon juice as they gave her a dim prognostic leading to being in a wheelchair within 5 years and possibly death.

The always straightforward Jackie took it in stride, maintaining her typical demeanor. "Ah well, I had a decent run! Solid 7 out of 10," she told Muriel "I will not be confined in a wheelchair, I would rather be dead."

Meanwhile, Muriel's dad Claude followed the news like a dark raincloud, slipping into a spiral of depression that left him utterly unable to function. Overwhelmed by fear and dread over his wife's condition, he retreated into a shadowy malaise - leaving Muriel to suddenly shoulder the full weight of maintaining the household in addition to her already heaping pile of teenage responsibilities. Sixteen years old and she was now the default homemaker: paying bills, grocery shopping with her bicycle, keeping on top of chores, all while still juggling school and... well, trying to magically help her mother through the mystic arts.

It was a comically lopsided distribution of tasks that would buckle even the strongest of modern juggernauts. But impressively, Muriel took this cosmic joke of a role reversal completely in stride, without so much as a dramatic eye roll or hushed whisper of "Ugh, baby boomers..." Her sole focus was on studying the ancient alchemical methodologies that would allow her to channel life's emerald currents into restoring her mother's spark.

Meanwhile, Muriel was having none of this diagnosis and prognostics. Her mom was not going to waste away into a twisted lump of atrophied limbs and bedpan existentialism, not if she had anything to say about it. Determined to act, she locked herself in her room for a few hours, dimmed the lights, sparked up some sandalwood incense, listened to spring from Vivaldi, and entered a meditative stage.

As her breath slowed and awareness expanded, Muriel opened herself to receiving the guidance of unseen forces. Angelic melodies seemed to whisper on the edges of perception, an otherworldly symphony coaxing her consciousness to shed its physical constraints. She felt herself rising, expanding, merging with a profound ocean of ancestral wisdom.

Muriel emerged from her trance utterly transformed, eyes blazing with inner knowledge and purpose. in this moment, floating on the ineffable resonance of the angelic symphonies still echoing within her, she immediately set to work…

What followed was a montage of routines that looked ordinary compared to the grand cosmic visions dancing in Muriel's mind. But she understood now that true healing came through small, grounded steps in alignment with nature's archetypal patterns.

With unwavering faith in her ability to inspire healing, Muriel crafted an unorthodox protocol for her mom - in favor of holistic practices steeped in natural rhythms and intuitive knowing. Herbal remedies, energy work, mindfully curated nutrition - these became the pillars of the chrysalis she wove around Jackie's failing body.

So instead of lifting weights or running up the Rocky Mountains, it involved:

Develop a nutrient-dense, anti-inflammatory diet plan to flood Jackie's body with healing vitamins and minerals. No boring health regimens are allowed. Muriel's Mom Makeover Plan demanded big flavors, big fun, and maybe just a soupçon of ruthlessly tricking my dear mother into prioritizing her well-being (all out of pure, innocent love, of course).

In the place of processed food, Muriel arranged an invading force of pulsing fruits and veggies in every color a hungry prism could fathom. Great orbs of cantaloupe and sunshine bursts of mango. Riotous fuchsia fireworks of dragon fruit and radishes so crimson they could out-blush a dramatic southern belle. With a stocked artillery of the earth's most vibrantly hued gifts, she was ready to fight her first battle: Mom's palate.

In a heartwarming display of love and creativity, Muriel encouraged her mom to embrace the art of knitting, recognizing its therapeutic benefits for both body and mind. With a twinkle in her eye and a playful spirit, she requested her mom to knit a long, heavy sweater adorned with a medley of colorful wools and intricate handcrafts. Not only would this endeavor keep her mom's hands engaged and nimble, but it would also provide a delightful mental challenge, fostering a sense of accomplishment and fulfillment with each stitch.

The biggest battle, though? Rallying my mom's diminishing reserves when her body begged for the reprieve of unmoving surrender. On those days when her muscles creaked like an ancient wooden ship and every step felt like trudging through soul-sucking quicksand, the last thing she wanted was her daughter forcing her into the next sweaty exertion. Going for gentle walks together, from walking in the yard to gradually increasing the time and distance as Jackie's stamina improved to walking in a forest with the dogs.

Of course, nourishing the physical form was only one plank of my holistic master plan. True vibrational wellness demanded reaching the deepest cores of mind, heart and spirit as well. This called for turning our humble abode into a resonance chamber effusing nothing but the most transcendently nourishing frequencies. Playing soothing music and reading aloud from uplifting books and poetry to create a cocoon of positive vibrations.

It was a holistic regimen focused on steadily rebuilding Jackie's physical, mental, and spiritual vitality from the ground up. No flashy magic tricks or elaborate rituals - just an integrated lifestyle overhaul rooted in consistency, patience, and nurturing the body's innate healing capacities.

Muriel was tweaking the protocols based on Jackie's unique energetic patterns, always attuning to the cosmic undercurrents guiding her work. While the process looked outwardly simply, she operated from a heightened state of awareness, seeing each choice and action as a sacred ritual in harmony with the universe's grand choreography.

Meditating daily, Muriel began peeling back layers of her self-doubt and conditioning to uncover a blazing core of confidence. The teenage girl subsided while a priestess of personal empowerment emerged, one whose sheer force of presence commanded life's rejuvenating currents to flow in alignment with her will.

Every day brought small victories - Jackie slowly regaining her vitality, her movements becoming more fluid, her spirit brightening. With each breakthrough, Muriel's connection to wisdom pulsing through all creation strengthened. She was no longer a powerless daughter at the mercy of cruel fate; she was an embodiment of the infinite potential that dwells within us all if only we can access it.

As her mother's condition improved with the help of a small dose of medication and the unique protocol outlined above, the realization dawned, that It had worked. Her New Age-y, healing protocols - the ones her parents and family had undoubtedly dismissed as the misguided ramblings of an overly energetic teenager - had somehow produced a positive change and outcome.

Sometimes, if the intentions are pure, it doesn't matter how crazy the path looks from the outside. The greatest transformations come from within, fueled by hope, dedication, and always...a little dash of teenage angst. Our bodies and minds are far greater than any doctor or cynic could ever fathom.

In time, the progress became undeniable. Jackie did far more than stabilize - she flourished, into her seventies with a zest for life. Looking at her now, alive, walking, cooking, and driving, you'd never suspect the grim prognosis that was given to her decades ago.

Muriel came to realize that the awakening she had triggered in her mother was simply the first blossoming of her unlimited capacity to heal, create, and transform. Her path was not one of subsistence but of continual rebirth into higher dreams and vaster potential.

Now a radiant beacon of self-actualization, Muriel shares the fire of possibility that burns within her, igniting others to courageously embark on their voyages of becoming. To those stuck in inertia and fear, she extends an invitation, one written in the unwavering testimony of her own life:

Let go. Say yes to the yearning within your heart. Become the hero of your transformational epic, again and again. For the only limits are those we impose upon ourselves.

All else falls away when we surrender to the eternal reinvention that awaits our awakened embrace. Just as she metamorphosed into her highest self to breathe new life into her mother, so too can we each emerge, Shakti arisen, dancing ecstatic reverence into this grand unfolding universe.

With every telling of her journey, Muriel's message takes on new layers of power and nuance. For she has come to understand that true transformation is never complete - it is an infinite unfolding, a continual unfurling into ever-deeper planes of wisdom and possibility.

Her latest emergence finds Muriel in the role of an elated healer transformational coach, dancing transcendent portals into being. At gatherings, she leads ecstatic movement rituals that rapidly accelerate the expansion of those ready to elevate to higher consciousness. Entranced by primal drumbeats, she emanates shakti frequencies that engulf the circle, inciting profound awakenings and triggering glimpses into one's potential as an infinite creative force.

Yet even as she assumes these roles of mentor and guide, Muriel knows this is merely one fleeting step in an eternal unfurling. True awakening is not a static milestone but a dynamic continuum of perpetual rebirth and reinvention.

So, with every dawn, Muriel embarks anew - returning to that space of the beginner's mind and opening herself to the next octave of wisdom, the next potent vision of what's possible. She surrenders in childlike trust to the governing forces shepherding her cosmic evolution.

"My only practices now are a complete embracing of wonder and a joyful curiosity for what the universe seeks to birth through me next," she shares, eyes brimming with mischievous twinkles. "For if I can go from a teenage suburban daughter to an intergalactic healing conduit in just one human lifespan, imagine what awaits us all when we simply say 'yes' to our limitless becoming!"

With that signature sparkle and insuppressible laugh, she is off again - thrusting herself into whatever transcendent adventure the eternal Now beckons her to explore. Always in transition, always in emergence, her very existence proclaims the divine message:

When the doctors deliver those fateful words - that cold, clinical verdict separating your world into the "before" and "after" - it can feel like the entire universe is crumbling beneath your feet. In those viscous first moments, choosing to embrace hope over despair is an act of spiritual bravery.

But I'm here to remind you, dear courageous one, that you come from an ancient lineage of metamorphic warriors - beings who have stared down inevitable transfigurations and chosen to alchemize the journey into one of transcendent renewal and rebirth. Within you dwells an incandescent ember of primordial medicine, a cosmic sarcode programmed to rouse your entire being as an instrument for radical healing on every level.

So take a breath, feeling your solar plexus expand. Tune inward to the relentless thrum of your heart. And know that the path forwarding is one of stepping ever-more-fully into the magnitude of what you are - a holistic conduit for rejuvenating states of grace beyond any physician's purview.

First, affirm: Nothing is objectively "terminal" unless you allow it to terminate the radiance burning at your essence. Whatever condition presents itself is simply the current isometric shape your soul has chosen to express and evolve through in this lifetime. But it is merely a vibrational construct - one that can be dismantled, transcended, and alchemized into a new harmonious instrument through your word, your focus, and your unwavering belief in life's infinite potential.

Then get creating, dear infinite artist! Build a healing world around your journey that serves as its resonant embodiment of the metamorphosis you're modifying. Let it be an alchemical shift environment infused with the elevated frequencies that beckon your revered one's spirit into its most vibrant, sovereign expression.

Mask all spaces in atmospheric symphonies of language tones or ethereal instrumentals attuned to nature's regenerative codes. Flourish them with the prismatic vitality of living botanicals and the glow of warm crystalline fractals. Anoint the very air with botanical tinctures and ceremonial resins to amplify your intentionality.

Then tend the ancestral heart of this healing homestead, stoking its emanations through the fires of devotional practice and invocations of divine regenerative will. Let every action be a sacrament to the inexhaustible wellspring you're drawing from, every ritual a fervent prayer to the holographic forces that govern physical rejuvenation.

And remember, you are never alone in this hero's journey. With every impassioned celebration of life, you join the celestial chorus of all those who've chosen reemergence before you. The transcendental melodies you emit serve as radiant beacons, beckoning benevolent forces across infinities to lend their ions to your cause. You are also bolstered by the lineage of Earth's primordial healers, the ancient mystics who divined the alchemical song lines governing renewal in all its myriad incarnations. Draw ever deeper from their coded wisdom, allowing their sublime verse to flow through you in healing torrent.

Most importantly? Refuse to relinquish an iota of faith in the vision that summoned you to this quest. Keep returning to the unwavering knowing that complete regeneration is not just possible, but the core harmonic driving all existence's eternal dances. Trust that the blossoming you behold in your ceremonies and meditations is simply the first crystalline glimpse of the full metamorphosis extending its sublime tendrils throughout all spheres.

Let that certainty be the eternal flame that guides you unswervingly along this path, radiant one. Because deep within, you know this was simply the initiation into your next phase of mastery as a shapeshifter of realities.

Tears may fall like healing rains; tremulous times may pass like thunderous storms. But like all cycles of death and rebirth, the horizon always holds the inevitability of new dawns, heralding your ultimate triumph as an infinite architect of life.

So, embrace this journey as the supreme rite of spiritual alchemy it is, dear cosmic friend. At its finale, the greatest transformation you'll behold is you, reborn as the supreme artist of worlds...then watching what new masterpiece blossoms when guided by your newly embodied powers.

"Keep blossoming, beloved ones! Transformation is the essence of life itself - so let us rejoice in surrendering to its rapturous upswell. For we are infinite, and our renaissance is forever just beginning."

Ken D. Foster

THE WORLD UPSHIFT MOVEMENT: UNRAVELING THE BUTTERFLY EFFECT

In recent years, a global awakening has been taking place – an upshift towards greater consciousness, interconnectedness, and sustainability. This movement, known as the World Upshift Movement, is gaining momentum as more individuals and communities worldwide embrace a holistic approach to life and well-being.

At the core of this movement lies the knowledge that every thought, action, and choice we make has the power to create ripples of change that can positively impact the world around us. This movement is closely allied with the famous Butterfly Effect.

As you may know, the Butterfly Effect is a term coined in chaos theory, which illustrates how slight changes in one part of a system, can lead to significant effects in another part of the system. Just like the flapping of a butterfly's wings can cause a chain reaction leading to a sunny day on the other side of the world, our individual actions and intentions can have far-reaching consequences in the interconnected of us all.

Moreover, the butterfly effect challenges us to consider the implications of our interconnectedness on a larger scale. In a world where technology and globalization have made it easier than ever to communicate and collaborate across borders, the impact of individual actions and decisions can be magnified, shaping the fabric of society and the world at large.

In this chapter, I will explore how science and nature are coming together to and forming a new paradigm which includes a combination of quantum mechanics, quantum physics, neuroscience, entanglement theory, Vedic scriptures, and practical techniques. By delving into these realms, I will be exploring with you new ways to expand your awareness and transform your life.

The Upshift Movement

For those of you who are unfamiliar with the Upshift Movement, it represents a powerful new force for positive change, with the potential to impact thinking, behaviors, and the planet on a global scale. This movement is rooted in the idea of personal development and collective transformation. It seeks to inspire individuals to ascend their consciousness, embrace sustainable practices, and foster a more harmonious relationship with Mother Earth and all who live on this planet.

By encouraging a shift towards greater mindfulness, empathy, and social responsibility, the Upshift Movement holds the promise of changing our paradigms and creating a more sustainable and compassionate world for all.

The Butterfly Effect and Quantum Physics

The comparison between the butterfly effect and quantum physics offers a fascinating exploration of how seemingly unrelated concepts in chaos theory and quantum mechanics reveal profound insights into the nature of the universe.

The butterfly effect suggests that small actions can lead to significant and unpredictable outcomes, highlighting the sensitivity of complex systems to initial conditions. Quantum physics, on the other hand, delves into the behavior of particles at the smallest scales, where the principles of superposition and entanglement challenge our classical notions of reality.

At first glance, the butterfly effect and quantum physics may appear to operate in different realms of science, one dealing with macroscopic systems and the other with the microscopic world of particles. However, upon closer examination, intriguing parallels begin to emerge. Both concepts underscore the interconnected nature of the universe, where the actions of one part can have far-reaching consequences overall.

In quantum physics, the idea of superposition suggests that particles can exist in multiple states simultaneously until measured, leading to a branching of possibilities akin to the multiple paths that can unfold from a small perturbation in a chaotic system. Furthermore, the concept of entanglement in quantum physics mirrors the ripple effects of the butterfly effect, illustrating how seemingly distant particles can become instantaneously correlated, implying a deep interconnectedness that transcends physical distance.

By drawing parallels between the butterfly effect and quantum physics, we realize the profound implications these theories may have on our understanding of the universe. They challenge us to reconsider our notions of cause and effect, separation theories, determinism, and the boundaries of classical physics, opening our minds and hearts to explore the intricate fabric of reality that we are only beginning to unravel. In this way, the comparison between the butterfly effect and quantum physics serves as a bridge between macroscopic chaos and microscopic quantum weirdness, offering a holistic perspective on the interconnectedness of the cosmos.

Entanglement Theory and the Butterfly Effect

The butterfly effect and entanglement theory are also two fascinating concepts from different branches of science that both highlight the interconnected nature of the universe, albeit in diverse ways. The butterfly effect looks at how small actions can have significant and unpredictable consequences.

On the other hand, entanglement theory, a principle in quantum physics, suggests that particles can become correlated in such a way that the state of one particle instantly influences the state of another, regardless of the distance between them.

While the butterfly effect focuses on the idea that seemingly insignificant events can lead to large-scale effects. Entanglement theory delves into our interconnected regardless of distance. It suggests a deep interconnectedness that extends beyond the physical realm. In the context of consciousness, entanglement theory implies that we are all connected at a fundamental level, and our thoughts and actions may have ripple effects that extend far beyond our immediate surroundings.

Despite their differences, the butterfly effect and entanglement theory both underscore the intricate web of connections that exist in the universe. They remind us that everything is connected in ways that may go beyond our current understanding, whether through the ripple effects of a butterfly's wings or the instantaneous correlation between entangled particles.

Note that in 2022, the explorers of Quantum Entanglement won the Nobel Prize in Physics. Alain Aspect, John F. Clauser, and Anton Zeilinger won for their work using entangled photons to test the quantum foundations of reality.

As we dive deeper into exploring these concepts side by side, we can gain a deeper appreciation for the profound complexity and unity of the cosmos, inspiring us to approach the world with curiosity, humility, and a sense of wonder at the mysterious ways in which all things are interwoven.

The Butterfly Effect and Neuroscience

The comparison between the butterfly effect and neuroscience provides an awe-inspiring exploration of how chaos theory and the complexities of the human brain intersect to shape our understanding of the world. The butterfly effect is congruent with the findings of Neuroscience.

At first glance, the butterfly effect and neuroscience may seem unrelated, with one focusing on the dynamics of systems and the other on the intricacies of the brain. However, upon closer examination, fascinating parallels emerge. Both concepts emphasize the intricate interplay of factors that contribute to the emergence of complex behaviors and outcomes.

In neuroscience, the brain is described as a highly interconnected network of neurons that communicate through intricate patterns of electrical and chemical signals. This network exhibits dynamic behavior, capable of reorganizing and adapting in response to internal and external stimuli, much like the sensitive dependence on initial conditions seen in chaotic systems.

Moreover, the concept of neural plasticity in neuroscience reflects the capacity of the brain to change and adapt in response to experiences, a phenomenon that resonates with the idea of cascading effects resulting from small perturbations, as seen in the butterfly effect.

As we look at the parallels between the butterfly effect and neuroscience, we gain a deeper appreciation for the complex and dynamic nature of both chaotic systems and the human brain. These parallels challenge us to consider how seemingly small events or fluctuations in neural activity can lead to profound changes in behavior, cognition, and mental health.

This is important to know because it is now known that we can rewire our brains, make better choices, and have more love and harmony with all. From the science, there is no such thing as destiny or fate. As the great systems scientist, and author of The Great Upshift book says: "We are not predicting our future, we are creating it."

Ultimately, the comparison between the butterfly effect and neuroscience encourages us to explore the interconnectedness of ourselves with everyone on the planet. It sheds light on the intricate mechanisms that underlie our thoughts, emotions, and actions. It invites us to contemplate the profound implications of these connections for understanding the complexities of the human mind and the world we live in.

From this scientific point of view, we share a sacred journey together, and as we begin to feel the inner and outer bonds of connectivity, we start to be part of the solution for the world and a living part of the Great Upshift Movement.

The Butterfly Effect and the Vedic Scriptures

In the Vedic Scriptures, which are the oldest scriptures known, particularly in the Bhagavad Gita, there is a recurring theme of interconnectedness. Drawing parallels of the Butterfly Effect, Vedic Scriptures, and Upshift Movement. These ancient texts originated from India and encompass a vast body of knowledge on spirituality, philosophy, cosmology, and how to transcend limiting thinking.

The Vedas emphasize the interconnectedness of all beings and the concept of karma – the law of cause and effect governing our actions and their consequences. Just as the flutter of a butterfly's wings can set off a chain of events, the Vedic Scriptures emphasize that our actions, no matter how small, can have profound effects on the world around us.

In the Vedic worldview, every thought, word, and deed is known to carry a vibrational energy that reverberates throughout the universe, shaping our reality and influencing the collective consciousness.

Interconnectedness, embraced by the Upshift Movement, encourages us to cultivate mindfulness, compassion, and conscious living to contribute positively to the world and create a ripple effect of change.

Moreover, the Vedic Scriptures emphasize the importance of dharma – righteous duty and ethical conduct – as a guiding principle for harmonious living and spiritual evolution. Many people see duty or rules stopping them from doing what they want, but truly universal principles in the Vedas are there to help one become a master of themselves, and live free. The Vedas also teach us to align with our higher self, by living our values and understanding who we truly are. This not only uplifts our energy, frequency, and vibration, but it also contributes to the upliftment of society and the world at large.

As we navigate the complexities of our modern world, the convergence of the World Upshift Movement, and the timeless wisdom of the Vedic Scriptures, we are offered a roadmap for personal growth, social transformation, and planetary healing. By recognizing our interconnectedness with all beings and embracing the power of our individual agency, we can collectively co-create a more sustainable, compassionate, and harmonious world for future generations to inherit.

Applying these Principles in Everyday Life

I have been doing spiritual, business, and life coaching for thirty-plus years. I have seen incredible transformations within people who are committed to doing their own inner work.

The practical application of upshifting your consciousness from the understanding of quantum mechanics, quantum physics, entanglement theory, neuroscience, the Vedas, Chaos Theory (the butterfly effect), and the Upshift Movement offers you an approach to profound personal transformation.

By doing your personal work, you will gain insights and wisdom. You will have greater awareness, better health, and make better choices, which will lead to greater success and a more harmonious life.

Additional Ways to Upshift Your Consciousness

1. *Positive Visualization*: Take time to quiet your mind and then get clear with what you want. Think about what is most important to you right now. Then imagine what your life will be like when you manifest this vision. What will your friends and family be saying to you? What will you be saying

to yourself? Also, do this for the world you would like to live in.

2. *Meditation and Contemplation*: Engaging in regular meditation and contemplative practices will help quiet the mind, deepen self-awareness, and connect with higher states of consciousness.

3. *Energy Healing Practices*: Explore energy healing modalities such as Reiki, acupuncture, Bowen work, Qigong, or sound therapy. These will help balance the body's energy systems and promote overall well-being.

4. *Gratitude*: Cultivating a sense of gratitude will align you with the higher vibrations within you. I suggest waking up in the morning and before you get out of bed, think of 3 things you are grateful for. This is a wonderful way to start your day!

5. *Set Clear Intention*: Clarity is power and setting clear intentions can align you with your goals, aspirations, and willpower. This will help you manifest positive outcomes.

6. *Personal Growth and Learning*: Hire a coach. Most successful people have business, life, and health coaches today. Also, set your intention to be a learner and a leader by engaging in activities that promote personal growth, such as reading, attending workshops, or seeking out mentors, which can expand consciousness and deepen understanding. You can start this journey by going to kendfoster.com and signing up for a coaching or mentoring session.

7. *Yoga and Breathwork*: Exploring practices such as yoga and pranayama (breathwork) can help you balance your energy, have better physical health and mental well-being, and enhance spiritual growth.

8. *Mantra Chanting*: Incorporating the recitation of sacred mantras before or during your daily meditation can create

a vibrational shift in consciousness, leading to increased focus, clarity, and inner peace.
9. *Affirmations:* Using high-thought affirmations can reprogram the brain, and increase concentration, energy, spiritual awareness, connection to the soul, and increased willpower.
10. *Mindful Living*: Cultivating mindfulness in your daily activities which will help you stay present, reduce stress, and enhance your overall quality of life.
11. *Service and Compassion*: Practicing selfless service and cultivating compassion towards others will foster a sense of interconnectedness and unity with the world.
12. *Ask Powerful Questions*: By asking questions such as: "What are three steps I can take today to increase my energy, vibration, and love?" or "What is a Quantum Breakthrough I am willing to embrace in my life now?", you will gain insights into your next steps.

In Summary

By recognizing the profound implications of the butterfly effect, we can cultivate a greater sense of empathy, responsibility, and mindfulness in our interactions with others. We can strive to make choices that promote positivity, harmony, and mutual understanding, knowing that our individual contributions have the potential to create a ripple effect of kindness and compassion that transcends boundaries and unites us in a shared human experience.

I pray you have been inspired by this chapter and reflect on your role in shaping the world around you. It is empowering to embrace the transformative potential that your everyday choices and actions will make.

It is not reality to think we need to be divided by nation-states, borders, race, class, religion, or anything else that tells us we are separate. The truth is we are one. By embracing this truth and living in alignment with our highest self, you will step into your power and cultivate a more harmonious and balanced existence for yourself, your family, your nation, and the world.

The Upshift Movement holds immense potential to transform thinking, behaviors, and the planet by inspiring individuals to embrace a more conscious and sustainable way of life. Through a combination of personal growth, community engagement, and environmental advocacy, Upshifters are driving positive change that has the power to ripple outwards and create a more just, compassionate, and resilient world for all.

As more people join this movement and commit to upshifting their lives and communities, the potential for impact grows exponentially, offering hope for a brighter future built on the principles of mindfulness, sustainability, and social responsibility.

Dr. Ervin Laszlo was nominated for the Nobel Prize two times, and I host the Upshift Conversations with him, which you can find at **voicesofcourage.us/upshift**.

The talks are profound! Some of our featured speakers include: Deepak Chopra, Greg Braden, Mariann Williamson, Neal Donal Walsh, Jude Currivan, Dr. Bruce Lipton, Lynn McTaggart, Dr. Ervin Laszlo, Ken D. Foster, and thirty-eight others who are committed to upshifting consciousness.

Thank you for your contribution to upshifting our world. I encourage you to pass this book on to those you love.

Paul Dangal

CHAIN BREAK

Many times, I wonder why I am so attached to these underprivileged children and why my heart hurts so much when I cannot help them. Why do I want to go beyond my way of trying to figure out how they can have a better life? Why has God chosen me to serve them?

I remember working in the US and earning a decent amount and still being empty and not satisfied. God saw my heart, and through miracles, he brought me to the same District where I grew up and this is my story.

My father was a very well known witch doctor in his area and was born into a high caste. The caste system is something that Nepal is still stuck on. Many people used to come to him in the hope of being cured or solving problems they faced in their lives. My mom gave birth to eight boys and only three of us survived. No matter how well known witch doctor my father was he was not able to save his sons. My father being raised by an abusive mom had his own very deep traumas; His father hanged himself when my father was just 20 years old. His father was like his friend so when he died my father did not know where to hold on emotionally. Therefore, he poured his frustrations and emptiness on all of us.

My mom is such a gentle-hearted woman coming from a loving family that was very rich and high in caste. She was the apple of her parent's eyes. Never being abused physically or emotionally. She was 18 years old when her brothers arranged her marriage with an unknown man to her. She had never imagined the life she was going to have with her new husband and mother-in-law. I was the youngest child among the three who survived and my childhood is so hard to write about and express what I have experienced.

My first clear memory of my life was hiding under a bed shivering and praying to all Hindu gods that I knew at that point, desperately asking all of those gods to stop my alcoholic father from punching and kicking my mom, I saw her being beaten every day and it was not a normal beating it was like somebody trying to kill. So many times my father ran away from home thinking that he had killed her and he would be in trouble. She was being strongly abused verbally and physically not only by her husband but also by her mother-in-law. We brothers used to run and hide when we heard the drunk monster (my father) because if he found us around he would hit us without mercy. Even when he was not drunk we would never know why he was beating us, he would find any small excuse to pain us physically and worse verbally. I still remember thinking I preferred him hitting me than abusing me verbally; some of the things that came out of his mouth were more hurtful than a beating.

One night after a horrible beating, she started to pack and walked to her parent's house, which was 3 hours away. I being the youngest one started following her, and we reached there around midnight. My uncles were not so welcoming to us. They decided to call my dad and talk with him about the matter and he came and promised not to treat her like that but nothing changed. This was not the first time she tried to escape I felt like she had nowhere to go but to face her cruel reality. I still remember this day as if it was yesterday, as always we heard our drunk dad shouting and coming toward our home and we three brothers started hiding from him. The inevitable happened. My mom was on the ground and we saw no movement or sounds coming from her, we got very scared for her and we decided to fight this monster, we did not care anymore what he could do to us but we wanted him to stop hitting our mom. My elder brother was 6 years old, my middle brother was 4 years old and I was 2 years old. We united and started the war with this monster. One of my brothers pulled his hair another kicked him and another hit him with a bamboo stick we were defending our helpless mom with all our strength and fear of losing her.

When he saw that she was not moving he got scared that he had killed her and ran from that area and we did not know anything about him for a whole year. Yes, we did not miss him at all but our home was still un-peaceful because my mean grandma made sure that her daughter-in-law and grandchildren would continue to be beaten and verbally abused by her. After a year, my dad called a town phone and asked to speak with my grandma we were somewhat sad to think he might come back into our lives. After a few calls and a few more months, he requested to speak with my mom. Somehow, he convinced her to come to the capital city of Nepal where he was working in construction. So we brothers were left behind with our grandma who was the same or worse than my father. She not only beat us or verbally abused us but on top of that, she would hide food from us, and hardly fed us. Due to that, I got severe sickness related to malnutrition. I was taken to many witch doctors but nothing improved I became so sick that she asked my parents to take me away from her before I died. Therefore, my parents decided to take me to the city so I could see a doctor and get well before I would be taken back to grandma. At age 5, I arrived in a very cold city with all the clothes I had which were a short and a T-shirt without any shoes or slippers. When my mom saw me shivering with cold she gave the little money she had to Dad and asked him to get me a slipper and a hat. That was my first slipper. My parents were working in the construction of a hospital in Banepa and since it was a hospital, many foreigners would come to volunteer. When they saw that I was being loved by foreigners and was given clothes, toys, and candies they decided to keep me with them and not send me back to grandma. Up until then, I had not received love from anybody. The attention of those foreigners was like water to a dry plant. My father kept drinking and beating us.

Jim H Bingman was an angel sent from God to change our lives. He used to carry me on his shoulders and take me everywhere he went. He was a loving father that I did not have before. Jim was the one who introduced me to Christianity and the need for a true God in my life. He wanted to take me with him to the United States and educate me there but something went wrong and I could not get my passport at that time, so before leaving, he promised my parents that he would sponsor my middle brother and me through school which he mostly did. That is how we were able to study until grade seven. From that point, other angels helped us. Slowly as I learned more about God, I fell in love with Him. He became my true friend with whom I shared all my pain and sorrows. I wanted to give my life to serve him in a big way in my country. I was on fire for God; I started traveling to the most remote villages of Nepal and shared the good news of salvation with them. Now my only goal and passion was to become a pastor. Every time I would preach, it felt like that was my purpose in life. However, when some big names in that church started persecuting me, soon they stopped me from preaching in our church or other churches around Nepal.

Once again, I was helpless and voiceless in front of these very influenced people. I felt I had lost the purpose of my life. The few times I went to that church after that incident I felt like a black sheep walking in a place I did not belong. When visiting churches in another area I was told not to come again because the influential people had ordered them to not let me in. That rejection was very hard on me because I grew up being rejected from home and school, and now from a church and I wondered what had I done wrong to be treated like this. My joy left me and I started living my life in survival mode. It was a very painful experience to witness someone taking your life dream away from you in a grasp. Being a teenager and feeling dominated unjustly I reacted in a rebellious way. I started searching for a purpose in life that I had just lost. I was tired of being put down, stepped on, powerless, and all because my parents were nobody and voiceless due to their poverty. That road led me to many wrong decisions. From being on fire for God to a rebellious young man. I could not even recognize who I had become. Now I had no father beating me but I was beating myself by treating my body so wrongly with addictions. I was a walking dead body waiting to be buried soon. I wished I was dead I wished I had never been born my wrestling with my thoughts would not let me sleep many nights. Inside the hospital in their residential area was the home where this missionary doctor and his wife lived, she was my mentor and teacher. She was always praying for me, she would visit my home and always did the best that she could to help in the need of my family. She was only the person in the world as there for me unconditionally. One night after a fight with another group I got deeply cut near my ear I didn't want anyone to find out so I went into their home and she saw my wound and told me I needed to get stitches so to go the hospital. She also asked me what I was doing with my life. She added you are such a powerful man,

God has a beautiful plan for you, do not focus on people, search for God and serve him. I answered her, "I am being stopped by all these people how can I serve?" She answered, "not everyone is influenced there are God's people out there, pray about it."

A few days after that I returned to her and said, "Yes I found a very remote area in Rukum, West Nepal." She helped me pay my bus fare and packed my food for the way. After 2 days on a bus and 3 days walking, I went to that village where there was no electricity or road. They had no health post or hospital nearby. Girls in that area were very abused and it was very common.

After serving there for a few months, I wanted to open a skill-training center and a Bible seminar. I started praying and our faithful God provided. We had its very first training center and an orphanage. The work grew very soon in other districts also. After working there for a few years, I went to Mexico and US for my education. However, I was already addicted to the feeling of serving needy ones, God called me back to Nepal to serve more needy and voiceless children. When returned I wanted to serve in the eastern part of Nepal not many people want to work in these areas because of the poverty and the low caste people are very common in the border of India and Nepal. Many children are very far from the reach of education. Child trafficking is spreading speedily. Currently, we have a training center where we teach and encourage youths to be involved in their society and to teach the children of their community for at least a few hours a day, since most of these children are far from the reach of school. We also train them to be the voice of the voiceless and the power of the powerless. We have a huge need to build a school and an orphanage it will be a game changer in the work we do. I was in Chrysalis thinking I had no hope, believing I was a loser, was good for nothing, feeling dark around me, preferring not to be born, with a thousand questions but all that I went through was God's way for me to become a butterfly. Being in a chrysalis was hard but now I can say it was worth it. Every struggling and suffering child is a butterfly to be. The harder the process prettier the butterfly God has sent his angels on my way repeatedly to help me to be who I am. I want to be that to these beautiful little children. Every time I see a child being abused, without proper clothes, slippers, an alcoholic father, etc. I see a small me. I want to be Jim H Bingman, want to be there for them unconditionally like that Doctor's wife was for me. Chain-breakers of a society are what we pray for.

Emmanuel Sananka

WINGS OF CHANGE: EMPOWERING THE MAASAI COMMUNITY THROUGH EDUCATION, MENTORSHIP, AND ADVOCACY

In the heart of the Maasai community, amidst the vast expanse of the Kenyan savannah, lies a tribe deeply rooted in tradition and bound by the rhythm of nature. For centuries, the Maasai have treasured their cattle and sheep, seeing them not just as a source of wealth, but also as the very lifeblood of their existence. Yet, in a world where tradition often clashes with modernity, the Maasai face unique challenges, particularly when it comes to education and empowerment. As a member of the Maasai tribe, I have experienced firsthand the struggles and obstacles that come with seeking education. In a community where formal schooling is often viewed with suspicion, I embarked on my educational journey at the age of ten, following in the footsteps of my siblings and peers. It was a journey marked by perseverance and determination, as I navigated the treacherous waters of academia with the hopes of breaking free from the cycle of poverty and ignorance that plagued my community. However, my dreams went beyond personal success. From a young age, I harbored a burning desire to uplift my community, to empower young people to treasure education as a path to a brighter future. I recognized the transformative power of knowledge, and I was determined to share that gift with my fellow Maasai youth. Growing up in a pastoralist community, I witnessed firsthand the struggles of my people. Limited access to education meant that many young Maasai were unable to pursue their dreams and aspirations. Instead, they were forced to rely on traditional methods of survival, such as cattle herding and subsistence farming. While these practices are deeply ingrained in our culture, they often perpetuate a cycle of poverty and dependence, leaving many Maasai trapped in a cycle of hopelessness and despair. Determined to break free from this cycle, I dedicated myself to the pursuit of education, despite the challenges and obstacles that stood in my way. With the support of my family and community, I enrolled in school at the age of ten, determined to carve out a better future for my loved ones and myself. It was not an easy journey, but I persevered, fueled by a burning desire to make a difference in the lives of those around me. As I progressed through school, I became increasingly aware of the disparities that existed within my community. While some children had access to quality education and opportunities for growth, many others were left behind, unable to access the resources and support they needed to succeed. It was a stark reminder of the inequality that pervaded our society, and it fueled my determination to create change. With each passing year, my passion for education and empowerment grew stronger. I became involved in various community initiatives aimed at promoting education and supporting young people in their academic endeavors. From organizing mentorship programs to advocating for increased access to resources, I sought to create a more inclusive and equitable society for all Maasai youth. One of the greatest challenges facing our community is the prevalence of harmful cultural practices, such as female genital mutilation (FGM) and early child marriage. These practices not only violate the rights of young girls but also perpetuate cycles of poverty and oppression. Recognizing the urgent need for action, I became involved in advocacy efforts aimed at ending these harmful practices and empowering young girls to pursue their dreams. Through education and awareness-raising campaigns, we sought to challenge deeply ingrained beliefs and attitudes surrounding FGM and early marriage. We worked closely with community leaders, elders, and parents to promote alternative rites of passage that celebrate the transition to womanhood without resorting to harmful practices. It was a challenging endeavor, but one that ultimately bore fruit as more and more families began to reject FGM and embrace alternative forms of celebration. In addition to advocating for an end to harmful cultural practices, I also became involved in efforts to address other pressing issues facing our community, such as early child pregnancy and limited access to basic necessities like sanitary pads. Recognizing the urgent need for action, I partnered with local organizations and NGOs to provide support and resources to young girls in need. Through initiatives like The Trueness Project, we sought to create safe spaces where girls could access education, mentorship, and support. We provided them with the tools and resources they needed to stay in school and pursue their dreams, including access to sanitary pads, reproductive health education, and life skills training. It was a small step towards creating a more inclusive and equitable society, but it was a step in the right direction. As I reflect on my journey, I am filled with a sense of pride and gratitude. Despite the challenges and obstacles that stood in my way, I never wavered in my commitment to making a difference in the lives of those around me. Whether through education, mentorship, or advocacy, I have sought to empower my fellow Maasai to dream big and pursue their goals with courage and determination. As fate would have it, our paths crossed with Dr. M Teresa Lawrence, the CEO of the Trueness Project, during her visit to Kenya as a keynote speaker. Her arrival brought with it a wave of inspiration and empowerment, as she sought to mentor and touch the lives of many young people across the country. Little did I know, this encounter would mark the beginning of a transformative journey that would shape my future in ways I could have never imagined. From the moment we met, M Teresa I recognized something special within me – a spark of potential waiting to be ignited. Despite the challenges and obstacles that lay ahead, she saw in me a determination and drive to make a difference in my community. With unwavering dedication and selflessness, she took me under her wing and became not just a mentor, but also a guiding light in my life. Through her mentorship, M Teresa shared invaluable wisdom and insights on various aspects of life, with a particular emphasis on financial literacy. She understood the power of knowledge and the importance of equipping young people with the tools they need to succeed in life. With her guidance, I delved into the world of financial literacy books, soaking up every bit of information and wisdom she had to offer. Nevertheless, M Teresa's impact went far beyond just financial literacy. She also recognized the untapped potential of Maasai women and the power of their artistry. With her keen eye for talent and her unwavering belief in the transformative power of art, she encouraged me to explore and embrace my creative abilities. Together, we envisioned a future where Maasai women could display their artistry to the world, empowering themselves and their communities in the process. As we embarked on this journey of discovery and empowerment, M Teresa became not just a mentor, but also a mother figure to me. Her nurturing spirit and boundless love enveloped me, giving me the strength and courage to pursue my dreams with passion and conviction. She saw in me a potential to change the world, and she spared no effort in helping me realize that potential. Now, as we eagerly await the Grand Butterfly March on June 29th, I am filled with a sense of excitement and anticipation. It is not just a march; it is a symbol of hope and transformation, a celebration of the collective power of individuals coming together to create positive change. In addition, at the forefront of it all stands Dr. M Teresa Lawrence, a beacon of light in a world filled with darkness, ready to lead us towards a brighter future. In M Teresa, I have found not just a mentor, but also a friend, a confidante, and a mother. Her unwavering belief in me and her selfless dedication to my growth and development have forever changed my life. And as we march forward together, hand in hand, I am filled with gratitude for the opportunity to be a part of something truly extraordinary – a movement of transformation and empowerment that will change the world for generations to come. However, my work is far from over. There is still much to be done to create a more just and equitable society for all Maasai youth. I remain committed to the pursuit of education and empowerment, and I will continue to advocate for positive change in my community and beyond. Together, let us spread our wings and take flight, dear reader, for the world awaits our transformation. As I look to the future, I am filled with hope and optimism. I believe that each of us has the power to change the world in our own way, through the small steps we take and the lives we touch. Like the butterfly that flutters from flower to flower, spreading its wings and bringing beauty to the world, so too can we make a difference, one small act of kindness at a time. I am committed to being a blessing to my siblings, my family, and the world around me. My greatest joy comes from seeing the people I mentor follow in my footsteps and make progress toward becoming the best version of themselves. Together, let us spread our wings and take flight, dear reader, for the world awaits our transformation. Let us embrace our unique gifts and talents, and work together to create a more colorful and compassionate world for all.

Shauna Sommer

BREAKING BARRIERS WITH BROKEN WINGS

SHAUNA SOMMER, THE GRIT COACH, OWNER OF GRIT GIRL LLC

As Maya Angelou beautifully stated, "We delight in the beauty of the butterfly, but rarely do we admit the changes it has gone through to achieve that beauty." This sentiment resonates deeply with me as I reflect on my own transformative journey and the power of grit in navigating life's challenges. Throughout my own journey, I have had significant trials that I have faced and during every one of them, it was the power of grit that allowed me to successfully endure and thrive.

At an early age, I was given the opportunity to see the intricately intertwined balance of resilience as it related to my own human spirit. I grew up in a small town that had a heavy mix of religion, a pilgrim spirit, and a healthy dose of ignorance to the outside world. This was both charming and challenging because my family did not exactly fit into any of the molds that dictated the norm for the area. Consequently, I had a difficult time finding my place as a youth. To top it off, my mother was a teacher in the community and my father was a truck driver; he was also an alcoholic. Because of this, I learned at a very early age that making things appear normal was a very helpful and practical skill to use when trying to avoid attention or criticism.

My home life would be categorized as dysfunctional to any outsider, but for me it was all I knew. Chaos became normal and consequently, when I was old enough to begin dating, I did not fully understand how to form healthy relationships. This led me down the path of becoming a young mother and marrying a man that was himself, dysfunctional and unhealthy. For nearly 20 years I stayed in a relationship that was full of trials until I found myself in my mid 30's desperately seeking any change that would make all the adversity I had encountered seem at least somewhat fair. Little did I know, the change I sought would find me and I would finally realize that if I was going to have a different life, a life better than the one I'd been living, I was going to need to make some drastic shifts in my mental, emotional, and spiritual state. This is where the concept of grit in my life truly began to take shape and although it was not necessarily intentional, I had developed a strong backbone due to my ability to navigate the trials and tribulations life had handed me.

The path I took was not easy, nor do I look back on it fondly. In fact, it is one I would strongly encourage any woman to steer away from. However, the education and training I gained throughout the first 40 years of my life provided me with more tools and resources to navigate challenges than any degree I have or could ever receive. In essence, resilience became the cornerstone of my capacity to not only survive but also thrive in the face of adversity. Like a butterfly, I emerged from my circumstances to transform into a strong, wise, and resilient woman.

Unfortunately, I have seen so many women like me, stuck behind a wall of doubt, fear, worthlessness, or simply not feeling capable of overcoming the hurdles they face. Have you ever found yourself stuck? Have you ever felt in your gut that you are not living to your true potential because your obstacles are just too overwhelming to work through? You are not alone! I believe that everyone has a certain amount of grit, and if you think back through your life, you can probably identify a moment or possibly more, when you felt backed into a corner and the only way out was to work through whatever you were facing. That's grit!

It may sound melodramatic to say that we all have moments where time stands still and the only outcome we can envision is a dire one, however amid adversity, it's difficult to see past the problems we are facing. Worry becomes a familiar friend and hopelessness becomes the lull we fall asleep to at night as our minds race with the endless possibilities of the negative outcomes our imagination can conjure up. Has this ever happened to you? Unfortunately, it is a place many of us visit all too often.

This is a destination no one wants to arrive at, yet many times our lack of awareness over our own inability to control the outcome leads us right to the wall we face. The reality is that control is a façade based on facts we have available to us at the time. Those facts can come from our experience, our education, or environment and yet somehow, we fail to realize that at any given moment the reality we know can be shifted. For example, if you lived in Florida, you could expect that hurricanes will at some point be something you will have to face. You understand the fact that you and your property could be impacted at some point due to your environment. You also understand, based on the education you have received, what you can do to mitigate the risk of damage or life-threatening situations, should a storm occur. Finally, you may have had hurricane threats in the past and none of them ever caused any significant issues. The reality remains that a hurricane is a powerful storm, and the intensity and location of its impact can change at a moment's notice.

I use this reference to illustrate that you can do everything possible to prepare for disaster, but faith is all you really have to rely on. I believe this and situations like it are those where prayer takes precedence over practicality, an idea I have defined as 'praying hurricane hard'. Essentially this is when you have done everything humanly possible based on experience, education, and environment to direct the outcome of a situation, yet you still ultimately have no control of what will happen. This is faith, and faith requires grit.

Without faith as the firm foundation for any plan of action we decide to take, we risk relying solely on what we know. If what we know fails us, we become vulnerable and at that moment, our mind becomes an equal playground for both good and evil. Awareness of this allows us to be mindful of unproductive people, situations, and behaviors that will not serve us well, it also creates an incredible space for God to come into our minds and hearts and produce some of His most magnificent work. I believe that is what breakthrough looks like. It's God taking our hand, or at times carrying us, giving us one tool after another, and helping chip away at the wall before us until we finally see the small light of hope on the other side.

Grit is demonstrated in resilience and persevere through challenging times, holding onto hope even when the outcome seems uncertain. The hope that is demonstrated during the navigation of difficulties is the reason I believe grit is more than a word to describe resilience and perseverance; it is a Kingdom word that stands for God Really Is There. Ruth from the Bible is an incredible example of this trait through her patient endurance and unwavering faithfulness, ultimately leading to restoration and blessing after a season of hardship and loss.

I have found in my own life that seasons of tremendous blessings often unfold after periods of immense struggle. It has also been my experience that the resulting lessons and tools we gain from those periods help to shape and mentor us in ways nothing else ever could. I have had multiple opportunities to find strength and courage in the obstacles I have faced.

When I was in my mid-thirties, I found myself walking out of the sliding glass doors of a hotel. I had just found out that my husband at the time was having another affair. As I walked outside, I pulled out my wallet and began taking out every credit and bankcard I had. One by one, I turned them over and began calling the 1-800 numbers on the back to report them lost. It was at that moment that I hit my wall. I was devastated, watching the remnants of a 20-year relationship completely disappear into a shadow of memories, heartbreak, and despair. All I could see before me was a huge wall that I had no idea how to go through. In fact, all I knew was that no matter how big and scary that wall was, and although I did not have a plan, I knew I was not willing to spend one more minute feeling helpless, hopeless, and broken.

That moment was a defining moment for me. At that point, I could have succumbed to the failure of a marriage, feeling unworthy of love, and willing to give up. That is not what happened though. For me that moment was not an end, it was a beginning and the wall that stood before me was not a stopping point but quite literally the opposite. It was the beginning of my 'what next', my why, my open door.

Overcoming divorce, death of loved ones, addiction and incarceration of family members, financial devastation, and heartbreak, I have had the rare opportunity to see the breakthroughs that came from each of those experiences. I learned that you do not truly overcome anything. In all the obstacles I have faced in my life, I was never able to go over, around, under, or beside them; I could only go through them.

Each stage of my life has been marked by transformation, yet it is the struggles and setbacks along the way that have truly shaped who I am today. From infancy to adulthood, I have encountered walls that seemed insurmountable and obstacles that threatened to derail my dreams. However, through it all, I have discovered the power of grit—the unwavering determination to persevere in the face of adversity.

To break through the obstacles, or walls, that stand before you it is necessary to understand that grit takes time, it takes effort, and it takes patience. I believe that it also takes faith, a tremendous amount of faith and trusting in divine timing and remaining patient as God works out His plans in our lives. This trust is demonstrated through patient endurance and faith in God's faithfulness, even when circumstances seem uncertain or difficult.

My personal transformational story is a testament to this resilience. From navigating the ignorance that pervaded my small town to overcoming unexpected challenges on my journey to adulthood, I have learned that happiness is not found in the outcome but in the journey itself. It is in the moments of struggle and growth that we truly discover our strength and resilience.

I am the owner of Grit Girl LLC and the creator of Find Your Grit Factor, a company and program dedicated to helping women show up; when all they want to do is give up. I believe in the transformative power of grit. The Find Your Grit Factor program is designed to empower women to overcome obstacles, cultivate resilience, and achieve their goals. I know that every woman, including you, is blessed with unique gifts and talents that only you possess. If you stay stuck behind the walls of obstacles you face, you will never allow yourself to step into the woman you were created to be, and the world will be robbed of the gifts you can offer it.

You only have a limited time here and time is something you cannot afford to waste. You owe it to yourself to take the journey of self-discovery and transformation so you may fully step into the incredible woman you are. Embrace your challenges, learn from your obstacles, and emerge as a beautiful, powerful force, full of faith and determination. This is YOUR life, it is time you spread your wings and fly. I would love for you to come get gritty with me. To learn more about me or how to embark on your own transformative journey, visit www.findyourgritfactor.com.

Jonathan Brierre

MOVING FROM FORCE TO FLOW - A JOURNEY FOR TRUTH, TRANSFORMATION, AND SURRENDER

Have you ever had a moment when you realized your life until that point was a lie? I know I have… on multiple occasions and circumstances, actually. In groping with the fabric of reality over the years, I have come to swallow some very bitter truth pills about life.

Perhaps the most impactful is the human ego has difficulty differentiating truth from falsehood. As a result, we are generally prone to being trapped and trapping others in karmic cycles created by our negative emotions and false outlooks on life. It is often only by the grace of God that we can grow from these experiences to find greater truths and principles to live by. Many of us never outgrow our preconditioned falsities and thus continue living lives of forceful suffering.

Ego Death and the Embrace of Suffering

I remember when I first reckoned with this truth many years ago as a freshman in university. I came into the experience thinking I was the king of the world and ready to become "The Black Dr. Phil." I intended to pursue a career in psychiatry and journalism; my heavy course load naturally reflected that. As I got further into my first semester, however, my mental health started to ironically slip. It was not until years later that a doctor officially told me I experienced a psychosis of sorts.

As a meditation teacher and life coach, I have found that it often takes great pain to springboard us into greater awareness. Our suffering in these crucial moments is the catalyst we need to let go of what is not serving us and transform into a more integrated and virtuous self. As a psychotic college student, I realized many falsehoods I would attached myself to.

To name a few of these falsehoods, I believed that I had to constantly perform and work for the love and approval of others. I thought that if I was not actively working to win people over, I was losing them. I believed that one of the only ways to have fun with others was with drugs and alcohol! I thought that my inability to keep up with my highly overwhelming schoolwork was indicative of me being a failure.

As I held onto these beliefs, my speech and actions naturally would follow and thus would influence the perceptions of those around me. I naturally came off as manipulative, disorganized, robotic, forced, and disingenuous. To no surprise, I ended up finding myself in a pit of despair and isolation. In retrospect, this was probably one of the best things to happen to me.

Although I had found myself in a self-perpetuating karmic hole, I decided to confide in a friend about my struggles. It was from our conversations that I learned about the benefits of meditation, and he introduced me to the works of Wayne Dyer. It also became evident that I was seeking beyond myself for things that could only be found within myself. As I learned more about mindfulness and spirituality, I devoted myself to studying spiritual texts alongside a daily meditation practice to find the peace I sought.

Inevitably, what started as a psychotic break had transformed into an equally scary and intense kundalini awakening within me. Before this happened, I thought I significantly understood who I was and where I was going. Now, I had no idea what anything was as I was so very full of crap, lies, and limiting beliefs. I began realizing that I had layers upon layers of trauma and societal conditioning to unravel and that being in college was not serving me in pursuit of greater wisdom.

So, against my parents' wishes, I decided to drop out of university to pursue spiritual enlightenment and worldly abundance! While doing so, however, I knew I was getting in my own way regarding these things. I also had not created enough momentum to manifest the life I wanted for myself. Therefore, to expedite letting go and reconditioning myself, I pursued a career in entry-level sales and marketing!

Even though I had horrible social anxiety and was terrible at relating to others, I figured that pursuing this career would be a great way for me to interact with the world and put my belief systems to the test. I wanted to push myself far outside of my comfort zone and become better aware of my patterns. That way, with awareness, I would be able to transcend said limitations and practice new ways of being and becoming.

Over the next five years, I dove headfirst into any sales position I could get my hands on. I started by getting my real estate license and receiving mentorship in real estate markets and sales in that domain. When I realized that was not a good fit, I moved to selling knives. Then I tried insurance, lead-gen software, retail sales, makeup, and cars... It was a long journey, to say the least.

The most impactful job I had was the one where I was selling makeup products. I recently wrote an article for Entrepreneur Magazine on this experience, and you can read it if you googled 'I Pitched 300 People a Day for 1 Year." Indeed, it was the most grueling and shaping experience, I have had to go through. In the rain, snow, and blistering summer suns, I was tasked to speak to 300 people daily about makeup. At first, I was terrible at it, but I became more natural as time passed. I started becoming a top sales producer in my office, and I managed to recruit a team of three other account managers at the age of 20.

Although I was finding some momentum in this position, I soon plateaued. The reason? More lies! I found myself running into some more false beliefs and thought patterns that did not serve me and kept me stagnant. On top of that, I was pushing 70-80-hour work weeks, so I had no time to process my emotions properly. Therefore, I inevitably was burned out and had to quit the job.

From that moment, I started grieving. Not only was I mourning the loss of this job and the goals I had doing it, but I was also grieving my loss of self. Once again, I was in a place where I had to face the question 'Who am I?" My beliefs about money and communicating with others still seemed ineffective, and now I was even questioning my masculinity and what it meant to be a man in today's world. So once again, I started searching for answers in books, courses, and from mindful contemplation. I also decided to take a less demanding job selling cars to help keep myself engaged in testing my beliefs in the world.

As time went on, I came to encounter and reencounter various other truths in life. One truth, in particular, changed my life completely as a car salesman...

When You Change How You Look at Things, The Things You Look at Change!

I think it is pretty funny how this one was crystalized in me... One day, I was making phone calls to different online leads the dealership had generated. I was being paid to bring them into the dealership so they could buy cars from us. I had recently had a rough month and was in quite a rut when bringing in new customers. However, that day, everything changed; my manager overheard me talking on the phone, came into the room after I finished speaking, and told me straight up, "You sound very boring on the phone."

My first reaction was to clam up and take offense at the comment. My manager did not tell me anything else or provide any feedback on how to fix the issue. Frankly, I did not like my manager either and thought she was generally full of it. Nevertheless, I realized that maybe I am the one who was full of it, and perhaps I should introspect and pick apart this feedback some more...

My inner dialog started something like the following: 'Me, boring? How could that be? Maybe this reflects something deeper within me... but what is it? Well, perhaps I should start with what I feel when speaking on the phone. What do I feel? Tired, lethargic, as if I was harassing these people and scamming them. I feel like these people do not like me and do not want to talk to me. I feel shame, a lot of shame... Are my perceptions truthful? Do these people really not want to talk to me? Well, they did opt into our forms to be contacted, and they are in the market for vehicles. Maybe I am being boring for no reason... Perhaps I can change my attitude and thus change my results here!"

That is precisely what I started working on doing. For the following month, I took it upon myself to write positive affirmations whenever I was at my desk. I would write out, "People are excited to talk to me and give me their money," and similar affirmations hundreds of times in between calls and on my lunch breaks. In adding this ritual to my routines, I naturally shifted my attitude and, thus, how people perceived me and the results I got. At the end of that month, my sales volume had more than tripled from where it once was.

That same month was also the last month I decided to work as a car salesman. At the time, I had predicted an apocalypse would happen the following year (when I say apocalypse, I mean in the etymological sense that alludes to great upheaval and revelation - or a mass veil coming undone). So, I wrote and published my first book, A Short Handbook for Happiness. I then enrolled in a software engineering boot camp. After 6 months of intensive coursework, I graduated the week Covid lockdowns started happening across the globe. Apparently, I was right on time for the apocalypse!

Because of the book I published, I found alignment with a nonprofit called the Leap Forward Community, whose mission was to spread emotional intelligence and self-awareness. I started building apps for them to support their missions while they also drilled into my unconscious mind. Funny enough, my work for them helped propel my engineering career leaps and bounds forward. My opportunity with them led to another and my current engineering contract for the past 2+ years.

The Art of Letting Go

Along the way, I moved out of my mother's house and found myself living on the beach of Far Rockaway, New York. If you do not know much about Far Rockaway, know that it is pretty far out - just about 2 hours by train to Manhattan. At first, I thought this was what I wanted - to live on this beach, without a car, isolated from everyone. But after a few months, I started getting depressed and lonely. In addition, I ended up sitting with this feeling and experience for 2 years.

Some thought I was crazy, and many misunderstood the reasons for my sacrifices. I did not have to live there - I made enough money to have moved sooner. However, deep down, I knew I needed to stay there and rediscover myself. In addition, that was precisely what I did. Through the pains, I found profound transformation as I sought the truth. After spending countless more hours studying the nature of consciousness and human nature, I could say that I firmly understood the underlying principles of human behavior and God's presence in reality.

It became evident to me how we often misunderstand what it means to let go and surrender and how it is usually a blessing to be able to do so efficiently. We find a relatively common occurrence ourselves in self-perpetuating cycles of negativity. Caught in the grips of despair, hopelessness, fear, lust, or anger, not everyone is ready to let go and embrace greater truths and realities. Not everyone is adequately equipped with the awareness of what that even means.

To help illustrate my point here, think of your mind as a still pond, and your emotional experiences occur as drops of water that hit the surface and ripple outwards. To let go and surrender implies fully experiencing our emotions, both good and bad, and allowing them to come and go. The goal of the spiritual aspirant is to get to a point where the experience of emotion is full yet momentary; the stillness of the mind is disturbed for just a brief moment and then let go. There is no clinging or attachments to our emotional experiences. To surrender is to flow with what is and to allow joyful things to be joyful and painful things to be painful!

Nevertheless, not many of us have the opportunity to entirely renounce the world and its attachments. Our lives are often stickier than what is ideal for perfect enlightenment, and that is okay!

Because of our attachments, our pains may sometimes come again and again, repeatedly, and again. In those moments, we must allow the ripples to come and, know that our stillness can be found between the waves.

For some of us, however, it may feel like its constantly pouring rain in our ponds, and we can find no peace whatsoever. I often pray for these people as they suffer the most among us. It often takes immense bravery to live through experiences like that while also keeping faith. Many broken people alive simply cannot do it, as their suffering is perpetual.

That said, the fact that you have read this far into my journey here now proves that you are amongst the privileged seekers of truth, ripe for transformation. Chances are, you are living a relatively stable life. You have a roof over your head. You have heat/AC. You are not starving. You have running water and electricity. No one is actively trying to kill you. You can access a relative sense of peace that most people alive do not have! While that level of peace may vary between individuals, you will have the potential to continue to tap into that peace for it to grow you, transform you, and bring you to your greatest version.

To follow the pathway of surrender is to thank God for all that is and to understand our lives as divinely planned and aligned. If you are unsatisfied with what is currently aligned for you, finding greater alignment implies leading a life of meditation, contemplation, study, and prayer. The deeper we understand ourselves, the deeper we understand the world. In becoming aware of our patterns, we can change them if we so choose. When we choose to change our thoughts, we inevitably change our values. When we change our values, we change our emotions and perception of the world. When we change our perceptions, we change our actions in response to these perceptions. When we change our actions, we can then change our reality.

Benvictor Makau Isaac

SOARING THROUGH TRANSFORMATION, A FLAP AT A TIME

Growing up, I used to admire Larry Madowo and his career life, marveling at how good he was and still is at his journalistic voice, especially because he has mastered the art of climbing the rungs and ranks of his career ladder, remaining at the top of his game.

As a young boy, I knew that if I were to snatch anything from him as my role model, I would have to work very hard, which is the premise of his success. Pairing this knowledge and passion with my strengths in languages, from a very young age, I was convinced that

I was on the right track. I kept moving, minding not much about the speed, but the direction. Every day, life's lights were shining brighter and lighting the goal clearer. The heavens favored me, and things were clicking into place.

I followed my passion, listened to my inner voice, sought advice, and prayed to my Creator for guidance and more indicators all along, and that's how I figured out the course I needed to pursue in the university—B.A. Linguistics, Media and Communication.

While still on campus, I could write for my blog and as a columnist for a certain media company, which I, one year later, joined immediately after campus as a full-time employee.

When I finally found myself at the office, having successfully been absorbed as part of the company's staff, it dawned on me that I had become a journalist! Yes, this reality defeated any doubts that my dream had been fulfilled. Maybe just like you, I had been admiring those corporate emails and I now had mine. It was my aha moment, and I gave myself a treat! However, that was just the start; it was barely the first day, and I knew I had myriad stairs to climb to become like my favorite Madowo, whose photos I had in my phone and to whose social media posts I would wake up, always reminding myself the much I had at the waiting bay. To become, I had to continue transforming.

The butterfly in me was no longer a larva; I had even defeated the pupa stage, and I was now a beautiful, adult butterfly.

This growth did not catch me by surprise, though, especially because I had been intentional all along, putting in the work, noticing the flowers budding and blossoming, acknowledging the continuous transformation I was undergoing, and entertaining a heart of gratitude. I reminisce about my life's stages with awesome wonder because I know that I am a product of resilience. Giving up has never been in my life's dictionary!

As a news editor at that time, still in my early twenties, the adult butterfly I had become had the responsibility of radiating beauty, bettering the world, and helping those behind me to realize their best versions and pursue them.

All of a sudden, I had become a leader, with followers behind me and mentees to nurture. I was in another phase of my life, a pathway to deeper self-discovery.

Every day we wake up is our golden opportunity to become better; it is a God-given chance to flap our wings more passionately and keep soaring higher and moving toward our greatness. "If you won't be better tomorrow than you were today, then what do you need tomorrow for?" asks Rabbi Nachman of Bratslav.

They do not speak like us, but we can tell that when butterflies are transforming, they undergo strenuous, uncertain, and, most probably, painful metamorphosis. Beauty is costly yet attainable. So is our transformation. As I continue transforming and seeking my best version, I have hit various snags. Uncertainty has been one of them. It's great and fulfilling to see yourself growing career-wise, getting exposed and connected, and finding clearer paths to greatness, but often a time, uncertainties creep in. "Where should I go next?" I would ask. "What's the next indicator that it's time for my next phase?" I would wonder.

I call to mind a chapter in my life when I was on the verge of giving up-yes, yet I still remember I have just established that this word is nowhere in my dictionary, but I was almost toppling. Growth, specifically growth intended to impact your life and that of others positively, is thorny at times. The journey to becoming is shaky sometimes. I wondered why I had been working my fingers to the bone, yet, in my opinion, at that moment, I had nothing to show for it.

Unknowingly, I had just turned ignorant to the inner growth, the resilience, the network, the goals, and the lessons I had nurtured. I felt like a failure; little did I know my chance to pass through the refining fire had come. I was being fueled to launch extraordinarily high.

Most times, we feel stuck and forget about the progress we have made, however slow. We start wallowing in self-doubt and seeing dark spots in the light instead of light spots in the darkness. We feel like our wings have, all of a sudden, become heavy on us, and fear of the unknown grips us. These have been other challenges I have wrestled with in my journey to becoming.

"So how did you dig yourself out of the miry clay?" you may ask. It is amazing how our faces shine and our shoulders straighten at the realization of our inner strength and potential and an understanding that we are on the loose, with all the power to achieve what we set our minds to pursue.

My experiences have been full of lessons that kept me going and from which I believe you would benefit. I share some of them below:

Transformation is intentional

Being intentional tops the list of the lessons I have bagged along the highway of transformation. No change happens by itself. You must instigate it. You must get out of the pile and do more than what is expected. You either disrupt or are disrupted. Even during the storm, I have always refused to be carried by the wave of despair because I know storms birth calmness. Never allow yourself to just flow in the direction life takes you. The oars are in your hands, and being intentional helps you choose the direction in which you want to row.

Mentorship is a gem

What a lifesaver! Mentorship takes you through shorter pathways without pricking your mind to this realization! You notice and evade the many stumbling blocks your colleagues have been stuck at. I cannot tell how my life would be if I had nobody to confide in when I am sinking and needing help. My lowest moments usually remind me of the gains of having a mentor. Like first aid to a dying soul, mentors are lifesavers! I confided in my mentor and sought advice because she had been, or rather, I expected her, to have had such a time in her career.

From groping for direction at the start of our conversation, the end was a grand idea, which I have been implementing and witnessing thriving. Adversity had just become a turnaround, and it was time to trust my metamorphosis. Thanks to mentorship!

Just take the first step

Martin Luther King Jr. noted that in life, "You don't have to see the whole staircase, just take the first step." Growth happens after you jump out of your comfort zone and start disrupting. This is where learning new skills, reading that book, taking an extra course, attending that webinar, signing up for that masterclass, and listening to that life-changing speech you have been procrastinating takes center stage. Your curiosity to learn and impact must remain insatiable. Most times, we put our lives on autopilot, sleep, and expect to get to our destinations!

Adversity is a gift

When you master the art of turning your adversity into an opportunity for greatness, you become powerful and unbeatable. I collected my pieces during the mentor-mentee meeting, embraced a mindset shift, and started nurturing unequaled positivity. I had been deep into the ocean, breathless, and it was time to bring out the catch. "I've never known anyone who said, 'I love problems,' but I've known many who have admitted that their greatest gains came in the middle of their pain," observed John C. Maxwell.

Understand times and know your passion

Over the years, I have not lived many though, I have realized that keeping in step with times and seasons sets you apart. Understand your life's clock; it will give you the tempo you need. Being a youth, I was keen to notice that technology was presenting so many opportunities to me and the bell was ringing for me to grab them.

I had realized my growing passion was in social media management, website content creation and management, and content strategy and editing, and I had many other skills I could leverage. "What do I have in my hands, and how can I use it to transform my life?" I soul-searched. Swinging into action upon realizing it was time to move from the traditional workplace environment and embrace remote work; I dived into virtual assistance and became a digipreneur.

Networking beats hardworking

I have come to so realize. You may work very hard, but if nobody knows you and your potential and you know nobody who can turn your life around for the better, you are walking in the mud in golden shoes. Networking is the new age we are in, especially when technology is threatening to make people estranged from their fellows. Apart from my faith in my Creator, leveraging mentorship, and putting in the effort with resilience, I have gained so much from the riches of my network. They have become my clients and collaborators, fellow change agents, and community builders in our zones of knowledge.

Self-awareness and personal development are friends

Beyond any wave of doubt, to transform into your best self, you must know yourself and your journey. Maya Angelou realized it and bestowed on us her wisdom: "You can't really know where you are going until you know where you have been." Know your strengths and weaknesses and understand what you do not know, then seek help in the form of advice and strategic partnerships and collaborations. Notice your passion and tirelessly pursue it. Hunger and thirst for knowledge and seek it by all means, and by that, you will be boosting your value proposition.

In my final year at the university, I took over fifteen certified online courses in preparation for my career, most of whose knowledge, exposure, and skills are propelling me to higher heights every time. I am still a student of life, embracing continuous learning, competing, and comparing myself with nobody apart from myself.

Maintaining a positive mindset, remaining resilient even amid storms, and keeping a never-ending faith have been my forte. I recommend it to you. We have been called to impact, transform communities, touch lives, and change the world by spreading love. Our skills, mindsets, gifts, abilities, and talents are our tools, and whenever we throw passion and love into the process, we become undeniably invincible.

Finally, be gracious with yourself; embrace direction over speed. Powerful transformation comes through patience and endurance.

Every day, I am piloting my life to higher heights, and because it is a learning experience, I agree with the wisdom of John C. Maxwell, "I'm not where I'm supposed to be, I'm not what I want to be, but I'm not what I used to be. I haven't learned how to arrive; I've just learned how to keep going."

Edinah Kangwana

THE GIFT OF PERSONAL TRANSFORMATION

*"The only person you are destined to become
is the person you decide to be."*

Ralph Waldo Emerson.

Transformation is a gift given to us human beings by the controller and harmonizer of the universe. I am a Christian and I believe it is a God-given gift to me, and so is to all human race. I am of the belief that, we were all created special and unique to fulfill a given mission and purpose on earth. However, the power to unearth this gift of transformation, live it, and be it is the work of an individual, it was not made obvious to us, we must strive to dig deep inside of us to find it, and once we find it, commit to work on it. When human beings do not embark on this divine journey of unearthing the precious gift of transformation, they get a miss in life, a void that cannot be filled by any pursuit; they live as empty vessels, with unfulfilled lives and untapped talents.

As Myles Monroe observed,

> "The wealthiest place on the planet is just down the road. It is the cemetery. There lie buried companies that were never started, inventions that were never made, bestselling books that were never written, and masterpieces that were never painted. In the cemetery is buried the greatest treasure of untapped potential."

These are the people who never took that one-step of unpacking self for transformation.

Through transformation, we become able *"To live the highest, truest expression of self as a human being,"* as Oprah Winfrey noted.

Born and raised in a small village in Kenya, Africa, a developing country marred with economic disparities and other inequalities making it challenging to access basic rights like access to education, decent shelter, three meals a day, health, and other social amenities. Coupled with the fact that I am a woman where women face in double the challenges that generally men face like gender-based violence, early child marriages, access to basic education all grounded in deep-rooted historical barriers housed by patriarchy. I know how it feels like surviving on one meal a day or sometimes none, I know what walking barefoot feels like, I know what being a teenage without access to basic sanitation products like soap and sanitary pads feels like, I know the anger witnessing gender based violence like partner battering, female genital mutilation (FGM), early forced marriages, knowing it is wrong but you lack a voice and the muscle to say no, I witnessed girl education in my country being taken for granted and women being denied the right to have a share to family property. I know what it feels being sent away from school for lack of school fees. I saw and lived it all. It is the adversities I experienced growing up, which propelled me to work very hard to rise above them. I leaned inward, tapping on the opportunity in adversity. I had no option, back then; I knew nothing about the free gift of transformation.

I studied courtesy of community and state sponsorship. Accessing this support needed a lot of growth inside me as a young leader, taking my life's destiny to my very hands, with hard work, integrity, honesty and deep roots in my spirituality. I always had to seek information, which was vital for my growth. I embraced the wisdom of mentors, sponsors, and collaborative partners. Above all, I clothed my soul with faith, hope, and optimism even against all odds. I know some of my peers who showed a very promising future but allowed their then circumstances of vulnerability, adversity, and disadvantage to mar their journey and are now living a life they detest.

Years later, I have the privilege of proudly saying I am becoming. I have had the honor of working in both corporate and public service for a period spanning over 2 decades and I am striving to be a change-maker in my community. I want to positively transform my community, more of being the very change I wanted to see growing up. However small, I am intentional in advocating for the power of transformation.

Transformation is birthed by the efforts of an individual. The environment surrounding us, government policies, the culture of the people around us, and the values of our communities become an added advantage and enabler for transformation. In this chapter, I borrow heavily from the butterfly transformation journey, coupled with other leadership development strategies and mindset, especially borrowed from the leadership lessons in the life of an eagle, to bring into perspective what individuals ought to do to achieve their personal transformation. Of more reference is my transformational journey, which I have been pursuing and I will keep on going. Below are some of the transformational strategies that have worked for me. It is my wish that they can inspire to action whoever is yawning to path his or her unique power of transformation.

Create a road map to your desired transformation.

Some call it a transformational strategy, others, a transformational framework. I call it curating your future story and roadmap.

We live in a world full of chaos, and diversities in opinions, perspectives and goals. We have many things competing for our attention; we also have many things, which influence our perspectives. Personal transformation call for the need to sieve self from all that and find yourself the clarity to achieve your desires and aspirations.

As a teenager growing up, I sure had and faced many distractions that offered instant gratification kind of solutions for instance getting married to the next available man who could offer me just the comfort of a decent home and three meals a day. I also had the option of sinking to myself, blaming my parents and myself and cursing God for creating me. I chose being a victor than a victim.

Even in my adulthood as I strive to become, I still face many distractions, even complex than before. However, I choose to focus.

You must know the ultimate goal, which is transformation. This can be a total life transformation or a particular area of your life that you think and feel needs a lift e.g. career, health, family, finances, or relationships. Draw a road map to achieving them. This is to say then that, a road map to transformation must start from a point of vision and mission. Do a current situation analysis of where you are and where you want to be, the gaps you want to bridge, your strengths and opportunities inherent in your transformation journey, your weaknesses and threats. Note what is standing on your way. Determine the outcome and then draw a road map.

Embody your roadmap with a great mindset, skillset and toolset, let the three be central. Develop a set of steps and strategies that empower you to unlock your potential, overcome challenges and create positive changes in your work and life.

Do not forget to write down your roadmap, our minds forget very fast; remember we started reminding ourselves of the many distractors. You sure do not want to fall off track or deviate to agendas not inline to your journey of transformation. This is your vision. Own it.

Trust the process.

The journey towards transformation is never a walk in the park. It is a long daunting one full of frustrations. Some days are good, some days are bad. The day for the breakthrough is not known, it is not a week, a month, a year, two years, or forever. Operate in optimism, faith, and hope for a better tomorrow. You have to keep walking, even when you cannot walk, or crawl. Working not to succeed now, but just that you are progressing.

Trusting the process prompts you to embrace the unpleasant life, your valley and plateau zones, and sometimes a lonely journey where you have to embrace and love solicitude. It is a process that calls you to dig deeper into the inner power, which only you know about. You will have triumphs here and there to celebrate, never fail to. Always wear a heart of gratitude, and count your blessings. The Bible tells about Moses and the Israelites where God ensured they got the necessities for each day. Most of the time because human beings want for today and tomorrow, we tend to ignore our present miracles.

As you transform, please celebrate them with gratitude. These moments add brilliance to the canvas of self-transformation.

Trusting the process also means allowing self-compassion when you fail, or when things do not go as planned. Remember the serenity prayer…"God grant me the serenity to accept the things I cannot change, the courage to change the things I can and the wisdom to know the difference."

Instead of beating and blaming yourself, own your mistakes and failures; take up those you can change and change them, those you cannot, own them as they are. Learn from the failures and build resilience muscle for tomorrow.

All that you are going through towards your transformation journey is building a very strong foundation for your transformation. Picture this; a stonecutter does not break the stone by the last hit to the stone breaking, but rather a compounded effect of all the stone hits that went into the stone earlier. Your transformation will be a compounded effect of all the wins and the failures you experience in the process.

A chick hatching process does not require the farmer to break the egg for the chick to come out; an attempt to do so will lead to the chick dying. You cannot force a pupa out of the its cocoon to make it a beautiful butterfly before its time, it will die.

Allow yourself to feel the pain, the discomfort. Embrace resilience for every masterpiece has faced various storms; it is a masterpiece because it survived. Have a positive mindset, avoid procrastination, and embrace goal setting and actioning of your goals.

Trusting the process means that you continuously ensure you are at your best in your mind, and embrace wellness even in the storms. Osunsakin Adewale noted, "After the storm, the sun will shine." You are able to enjoy the sun and the storm in your journey to transformation.

Continuous personal development.

Transformation is a continuous life process. It calls for a heart of humility that knows, no one knows it all, we learn from each other, from our experiences, all the time.

> "I am a fool, but I know I am a fool and that makes me smarter than you," Socrates

The philosopher's thinking above, that we know nothing; I know not all. We should therefore be committed to continuous learning, self-reflection and adaptation to new dynamics. It is an aspect of staying open and flexible to new insights, new perspectives, and new thoughts and adjusting to them. Always embracing a cup that is half-full ready to fill from the overflow of what the world offers, and continuously stopping to look and reflect on the content of your cup.

To be a vessel of transformation, one must be ready to put in the work to continuously learn from everybody and everything, from giving self to reflecting on happening around yourself and the world around you, the triumphs and the failures.

Go to school or college, get that one more certificate, and learn that skill that you think can be beneficial to you in the era you are in and the changes you anticipate to see soon. Attend that webinar or conference online, go to YouTube and listen to the many audios and videos free of charge, and follow social media spaces of people who inspire you in your respective career or passion. See what they are into and learn.

Embrace the culture of book reading, magazines and other reading materials. There are both audio versions of books even e magazines.

> "There is more Treasure in books than in pirate's loot on Treasure Island," Walt Disney.

We are living in an era where access to education has been made easier by technology, now than before you can do your degree online from the comfort of your home, cross-country learning, or different time zone learning. Indeed the COVID-19 pandemic gave us the gift of versatility in learning and connecting.

Continuous personal development is a strategic tool in personal transformation. It makes you opportunity-ready and builds your capacity to be able to handle the responsibilities after transformation, because transformation itself is you rising beyond the ordinary, souring high from where the rest are concentrated.

Your Tribe.

Your tribe are the people you hold dear and close to you. It is made up of your friends, family, mentors, coaches and sponsors. It is important to have a select group of people who can give you a shoulder to lean on when the burden is heavy, a handkerchief to wipe your tears when the tears roll down, and a pat on your back that, hey I got your back.

I call these people your tribe. They can be your family, colleagues who will sit in for you, support and understand you, especially in your low moments. Friends (even if one or two) who can honestly take a bullet for you.

Your tribe can also be people who have gone ahead of you in an area you are looking forward and working to transform yourself in. Can be in your career, family, finances, and relationships and they are willing to allow you to walk through their lenses. Telling you their success stories and even their mishaps along the way. They make your journey shorter than theirs. We call these persons mentors. One thing to always note is that mentors do not do the work, mentees (you) do.

In the same tribe group, you can have people who have the muscle to sit in tables and spaces that you are currently not able to sit on. These people because they believe in you, will say your name in these tables when opportunities come calling.

In your tribe, you can have another category of professionals like a coach and a psychologist. A coach will hold space for you to dig deeper to evoke your awareness and the inner power to take charge of your life while a psychologist will help you take charge of your health and wellness journey amidst all the storms life will throw you.

Another group of professionals needed in your tribe can include a banker, doctor, insurer, investor or even tours and travel expert. Onboard them in your transformation journey as the need arises.

Remember you are on a journey only a few have decided to be intentional about. Eagles do not fly high above the storm with owls.

Networking.

Do not stay in your cocoon. We love the butterfly story so much, but we (you) are not a butterfly. You are a human being given dominion by God, the dominion of greatness... So you can do better even than a butterfly story which we love so much. Go out there and meet people whom you think interest you, join in conversations that warm your heart, connect with people of your kind in the social media spaces...create friends, allies, role models, and mentors... all these will add to your social capital and we all know that your networks, also contribute to your net worth value.

Be strategic in your networking; first impressions are key, and when you get the opportunity to voice ooze wisdom. Selfie-taking with prominent people is not networking; not all celebrities can be of help to you. Be very intentional and strategic.

Collaborative partnerships.

Strategic partnerships are strategic tools to achieve a higher, bigger and impactful spectrum of whatever course you are advancing, including your personal quest for transformation. Be flexible and strategic, with open eyes, and glean from people of substance. Always strive to add value to that collaborative journey. Go cross-community, cross-border, cross-nations, and cross-disciplines.

Collaborative partnerships are meant to onboard diversity and inclusivity. You can have A and you need B. You do not have to be an A and B but you can partner with B and even C, to achieve your goals.

Share your story and light other candles.

Your transformation story is a seed of transformation to your generation and the generations coming. Be authentic by deliberately planting it and allow it to sprout. Others call it lighting other people's candles so that we increase the light in mother universe, for many candles shine brighter than one candle. One candle risks bringing total darkness to the world if by accident the wind blows its light off.

Tell your story of transformation to the world to inspire others. Share your journey, the struggles, the triumphs, and the invaluable lessons. As you paint your narrative, you contribute to the collective journey of transformation. Your story is a masterpiece and a testament to the resilience and infinite possibilities inherent in every one of us.

However, hey you, who can tell your story better than yourself? Trust me, nobody.

Take advantage of the opportunities social media spaces are giving us today. Tell your story of transformation, let authenticity and vulnerability be at the center. Public speaking engagements or even authoring a book. There are sure so many ways to tell it.

I picked the seven above strategies for they have helped me in my transformation journey. You, my dear reader need to note that there is nothing cast on stone; feel free to experiment, merge and even curate your strategies. Whatever works for you is great. Our respective journeys of life and transformation are great, but unique to every individual ... our differences lies in that uniqueness. The very thing that we ought to celebrate, because our differences are our strengths.

My last strategy is;

Ask, Seek, and Knock.

Take this as contemporary as so...however, for the Christians reading, this philosophy is in the bible too (Mathew 7:7)

Ask and you will receive, seek and you will find, knock and the door will be opened for you.

My dear reader, you have the innate ability to become, but you lack one or two.... The mindset tool, the toolset, or the skillset, and it is all right. Humans depend on each other. Do not die alone, reach out.

The worst that can happen is getting a no, not finding, and the door not being opened. None of these has ever killed anybody. Look at the other side of the coin; you may get a yes, find what you are looking for or, the door be flung wide open.

Rise up and be transformed.

Janice Burt

ONE FEAR PER YEAR

I am standing on a stage wearing high heels and a sequins blue bikini trying my best to flex my back muscles in the way I had been taught. There are 5 judges sitting in the front row studiously scrutinizing my every move, and the competitor who had just gone out before me in this bodybuilding competition was very blonde, very beautiful, and had legs that went all the way up to the ceiling. I swear, they just kept going. In addition, here I was, my short, sticky, shaking, and spray tanned body doing its best to walk across the stage and not trip and fall on my face.

I was terrified.

You might be wondering, "Well, Janice, if you're so scared of competing in this bodybuilding competition, why did you voluntarily sign up to compete in one?"

That is a great question! I have a pretty good answer.

It is because I was breaking free. I was breaking free from a life trapped in fear, people pleasing, and body image issues. Fear had become like a prison for me. It held me back. It silenced my voice. It kept me small and paralyzed.

After my 14-year marriage ended in divorce, I made an intentional decision that I was going to face my fears. I was tired of fearing controlling my life. I was tired of caring so much about what other people thought about me. I was sick of being a doormat and allowing people to walk all over me.

The loss of my marriage was the most painful, heartbreaking experience for me. I was codependent, so losing my husband felt like losing an arm or a leg, a part of myself. I could not imagine being able to survive a life without him. You might not be able to relate to a divorce, but my guess is that you have had your own traumatic loss. It could've been the loss of a loved one, the loss of your innocence, the loss of a dream, the loss of your health, or the loss of a career, just to name a few.

Loss and change are a part of each of our lives. They can help us grow or they can cause us to be bitter and angry. Ultimately, the decision is ours.

After my divorce, I blamed others for a while (my dad, my husband). I was in so much emotional pain that I could not think of anything else to do but blame and point the finger. After some time of feeling like a victim, I realized that having that mentality was not really helping me feel better. I still felt stuck and miserable. I still wanted to be rescued. I was still looking to the outside world to define my inner landscape. I was still waiting for someone or something else to complete me.

Given this awareness, I came to a different conclusion. I concluded that I was the common denominator in my life, and that *I* was the one who needed to change. After all, it really was the only thing I actually had control over.

I decided to do one thing that scared me every single year. One Fear per Year. It was an aha moment for me! I was going to walk through one fear each year and every fear that I bravely faced would teach me something, would empower me, and would build my self-confidence. I needed to do something drastically different from what I had been doing up to this point. I needed to approach my life in a completely different way.

It has been 12 years since my divorce, and these are the activities that I was really scared to do that I did anyway:

1. Ran a marathon.
2. Joined Toastmaster and started speaking my truth.
3. Self-published a memoir
4. Auditioned and acted in a short film.
5. Went to a 2-week yoga teacher training where I learned to meditate.
6. Competed in a bodybuilding competition.
7. Traveled to Spain and walked the Camino de Santiago.
8. Did stand-up comedy.
9. Joined a dance group and performed during half time at a Kings game.
10. Competed in a 40's plus beauty pageant in Vegas.
11. Participated in a Kenya Keynote tour speaking to thousands of students in Africa.
12. Bought an investment property in Georgia.

Every time I did one of the above-mentioned activities, I was really scared. However, my **why** overpowered the fear. I made the vow to walk through my fears because I knew they were holding me back from becoming the best version of myself. The thing I cared about above all else was breaking free from that prison of fear to be able to live the amazing, purposeful life that I knew was meant for me.

I hope you will decide to try this for yourself. The feeling of freedom you will experience, the authenticity you will embody, and the joy you will feel deep down is SO worth the effort of facing your fears. If you would like to join me in this empowering adventure of walking through One Fear per Year, I have a couple of steps to follow that will make the process a little bit easier.

Step #1: Prepare yourself for feelings of discomfort.

You will probably feel the urge to run in the complete opposite direction when walking through one of your fears. This is very normal and natural. You must prepare yourself for these feelings. You will feel uncomfortable. You will feel like you want to run for the hills. This is the exact moment that you keep going. You step out in faith. You "faith it till you make it". Trust that this process works and that you will experience true love and acceptance on the other side of walking through the fear.

Step #2: Chose an activity that you have always wanted to do but have not done because of the fear. Alternatively, choose a fear that you have struggled with and find an activity where you will have to face that fear.

Maybe you have always wanted to speak publicly or perform in front of a group, but fear of judgment and criticism has held you back. Maybe you want to walk through your fear of judgment and criticism, so you look to participate in an activity like public speaking, a performance, or a competition. It works from either angle!

Here are some suggestions of activities you could do:

do improv, sing karaoke, have a hard conversation with a loved one, go to a party and start as many conversations with strangers as you can, learn to play a new sport, work remotely and travel for a few months, write an article to publish, audition for a play, learn to meditate, go to therapy, get on a game show, volunteer to speak publicly, get sober, sign up for any type of competition, travel solo, go backpacking in the mountains, run a race, take a math class (if you hate math), take an English class (if you hate writing), make a new friend or end a toxic relationship. The sky is the limit! Use your imagination and go for something that challenges you.

Step #3: Set the date and mark your calendar.

It is really important to have a date for the event or activity you are doing and mark it in your calendar. You have 364 days to complete the task, so hopefully it will not feel overwhelming. If you are doing something like a speech, a performance, or a competition, the date will already be set for you, so you simply have to add it to your calendar. If, however, you are doing something that does not have a specific date attached, you must set the date yourself. Let's say that the fear you are walking through is fear of rejection or abandonment and you decide to have a hard conversation with a loved one, gauge how much time you will need to prepare yourself to have this conversation, and then mark your calendar.

Step #4: Tell at least one other person and join an accountability group or get a coach/mentor.

Everything I have done has been with the support of either one person or a group of people. I have not walked through a single fear without accountability and guidance. When I ran the marathon, I joined a training group. When I decided to speak publicly, I joined

Toastmasters. When I competed in the bodybuilding competition, I hired a coach. To really stretch outside of our comfort zone, we need help from others. We need encouragement and inspiration. We need support and motivation. We are better together!

Step #5: Remember your why and take consistent steps toward your goal.

Take time to remember why you are walking through your fears. Know that short-term discomfort is much better than long-term regret. Fear impacts us all. It does not matter if you are roaming the street with no home, or you live in a mansion overlooking the ocean. Fear impacts us all! It is up to each one of us to make the decision to break free. It is up to us to put in the effort and hard work on the front end, so that we can experience a life full of peace and purpose on the back end. As we walk through our fears, we make it possible to uncover the love within. It is this LOVE that will change the world. Love and fear cannot coexist. It is one or the other.

You do not need fancy degrees or years of study. You just need to choose courage.

Let's say you decide to tackle public speaking. People are not scared of public speaking in and of itself. The fear comes in when they think of the possible judgment, criticism, and/or failure that public speaking can provoke. As you tackle this fear, you will develop more respect and admiration for yourself. This in turn, will allow you to not care so much about what others think about you. You set yourself free from needing to get validation and approval from external sources to feel good about yourself. You feel good about yourself because you did something hard. You kept a promise you made to yourself. You stepped up and accomplished something significant. Yay you!

Here are a few of the outcomes you will experience after walking through fear:

1. You will have amazing stories to share with others.
2. You will learn so much about yourself through the process.
3. You will grow mentally and emotionally.
4. You will feel a sense of accomplishment and respect for yourself.
5. You will have unexpected revelations and insights.
6. You will feel lighter and more resilient.
7. You will be able to encourage others to do the same.
8. You will have an adventurous, fun, and exciting life.
9. You will lean into your own authentic expression.
10. You will uncover the LOVE within and be set free.

When you first start walking through one fear per year, it will be considerably harder than after you have been doing it for a while. Once you have trained yourself to consistently walk through fear, it will get easier. You begin to trust yourself more. You start to take yourself less seriously. You care less about what other's think and say about you. You feel pretty good in your own skin. You know that perceived failure is simply a step in the growth journey. You give yourself grace. You build your self-love. You realize that you are capable of far more than you ever imagined possible. You trust. You surrender. You accept. You gain awareness that you are here for more.

Early on in my journey of walking through fear, I wrote a poem that has reminded me throughout the years of the significance of choice. At the end of the day, there exist two choices: fear and love. Fear holds us back and love sets us free. We must each choose wisely.

Fear, the worst four-letter word I know.
It took away my dignity, my passion, my drive.
It left me cold, aching, and dying inside.
Fear, the worst four-letter word I know.
It caused me to doubt, and it caused me to suffer.
No, that's not quite right since I chose it as a buffer.
I wanted to protect myself from hurt,
And so, I let fear control Janice Burt.
But while lying broken and stripped on the floor,
I decided, through tears, that fear
would be welcome no more.
And instead, I chose another four-letter word.
Love is a better bet, that's what I had heard.
It turns out it's true, what they all say.
Replacing fear with love left me peaceful all day.
Love, the best four-letter word I know.
It gave me joy, happiness, and set me free.
It had me laughing and smiling, feeling good to be me.
It is always a choice, and we make it every day.
Why don't we all send fear out?
And invite the word LOVE to stay.

Walk through one fear per year and watch your life transform right before your eyes! You will let fear know that you are in control of your life, and love will be leading the way from this moment on. As we each transform, so the world will follow.

I believe in YOU.

Chris Murillo

THE QUEST FOR PERFECTION

As I stand in the bustling market of Tamarindo, the vibrant colors and exotic aromas of fresh produce surround me. I carefully select each ingredient, envisioning the culinary masterpieces I will create for my guests today. This is my daily ritual, the foundation of my craft as a chef.

I am Christopher Murillo, a 30-year-old chef and the host of the Costa Rican Culinary Scene Podcast, "A la Perfeccion." My journey to this moment has been one of passion, discipline, and the relentless pursuit of perfection.

Born in the beautiful island nation of Costa Rica, I was raised in a humble family. My early years were filled with the wonders of this paradise, exploring beaches and immersing myself in nature alongside my grandparents. While my parents worked tirelessly to provide for us, I found solace and guidance in the loving arms of my abuelitos.

My grandfather and I shared an unbreakable bond, strengthened by our love for soccer. The hours we spent kicking the ball and laughing together were some of the happiest moments of my childhood. However, as I entered my teenage years, my world was shaken by my parents' divorce. The pain and confusion sent me spiraling into a deep depression.

It was during this dark period that my grandmother's love and wisdom shone through. She taught me the value of self-discipline and the importance of channeling my emotions into something constructive. With her encouragement, I discovered my true calling in the culinary arts.

I threw myself into my studies at the Gastronomic Institute, absorbing every bit of knowledge I could. The kitchen became my sanctuary, a place where I could express my creativity and find solace in the precision and artistry of cooking. It was here that I began to understand the true meaning of perfection in one's craft.

Fast forward to the present day, and I find myself as the head chef in Tamarindo, having worked at prestigious resorts like the Four Seasons and the Doubletree by Hilton. Each morning, I meet with my guests to discuss their culinary desires for the day. It is my mission to create an experience that is truly "a la perfeccion" for each and every one of them.

Through my podcast, I invite listeners to join me on this daily journey, from selecting the freshest ingredients to crafting beautiful dishes and setting the perfect table. I share my thoughts on the importance of self-reflection, discipline, and the continuous pursuit of learning and growth.

However, perfection is not limited to just one aspect of life. My wife, Angelica, and our son, Job, are the anchors that keep me grounded and remind me of the importance of balance and love. They are the reason I strive for excellence in all facets of my existence.

As I stand here in the market, I am filled with gratitude for the journey that has brought me to this point. The quest for perfection is not just about the result; it is about the love and dedication we pour into every step of the process. It is about finding joy in the small moments and cherishing the people who support us along the way.

With a smile on my face and a heart full of passion, I begin my day, ready to create culinary magic and share my love for food with the world. This is my story, my quest for perfection, and I invite you to join me on this flavorful adventure.

Obed Charles

THE BLESSED TOUCH

In life, we meet people who perceive the gift of goodness in us. They provide us with the potential to conquer and rise above generational limitations. You have all heard the saying, 'A friend in need is a friend indeed.' I cannot take these words lightly. They expand our thinking ability to determine who is a true friend in life. To be considered a true friend, one must have gone beyond what life offer to provide moral support, mentorship, or emotional support throughout one's darkest moments. You know what? Friends may always be discovered in your call logs, not your phone book. How often do you reach out to your friends?

There are times in life when unexpected guest becomes the closest person to your heart. He/she transforms your life's bitter story into an intriguing chapter in your life. How do we call them? God sent? Angels? Pacesetter? Mentors? Whatever name you call them, believe me, they touch your soul, create your soul, and make a positive difference in your life. Where your possessions are, that is where your heart resides. That means your heart has the ability to guide your steps.

Growing up, I aspired to be a music producer and a great vocalist in Kenya. I could admire renowned performers in our country and envision myself among them. I pictured everything and assured myself that one day I would be a famous music producer. My beginning point was in high school. Soon after joining form one, I felt so small and scared. We had rigorous school captains in several sections who would chastise us when we went wrong. Overcoming fear was one of the tests I excelled at. Therefore, at form one orientation, I overcame my nervousness and played my favorite instrument, a keyboard. It was a fantastic experience, I tell you.

Everyone applauded me, and during that week, I became the topic of conversation among my fellow students at school. I told myself that I would improve my musical skills and lead my fellow classmates. After a year, I was the Christian Union's choirmaster, house captain, and our school's music club chairperson. I held these responsibilities until my senior year of high school. During that time, I made significant contributions to the school's history. My ambition for higher things gave rise to a career in music. It signaled a new beginning.

Returning to life after high school, I enrolled in the Highland School of Music & Audio Engineering in Tanzania's capital, Dar es Salaam. I came to Tanzania with one goal: to shape my music career. I was always at the top of my class. My tutor, Richard Mloka, hired me as an employee at the college's recording studio just three months after enrolling. He handed me the keys to the studio, which meant I had more time to practice my skills. The greater your imaginations are, the more profitable ideas you generate, and that is how WITO RECORDS was founded.

I was new to Facebook when I visited Dar es Salaam in 2013. It was the age when smartphones were first introduced to the market. Ambassador Dominic Obadiah was there to make a difference in my life. He sent me a message. It read, "Hello, Obed?" How are you? I hope you are doing great in your academics. I recently founded an organization and hope to implement the same approach in Tanzania. Will you be my contact person? I assure you it was a surprise, and of course, I accepted.

At that time, I had no idea how resourceful I was. I had no idea I would one day be a humanitarian rather than a music producer. When Ambassador Dominic Obadiah taught me about life coaching, I pondered what I would coach, as the only coach I knew was a football coach. (Laughing)

He saw something in me that no one else had seen before: leadership Abilities. An African proverb states that what an elderly person sees while seated it is hard for a teenager to see while standing. To summarize, I have worked as Dominic's personal assistant for nine years and have never regretted it. He has touched my life, my family, and many others in my country. He is my pacesetter, and I am grateful for the opportunities he has given me.

2023 began with a low tone. I was struggling financially, and my son Javier was just four months old. My daughter was in fifth grade. I could pray every day with my wife. When you are going through difficult times in life, you pray emotionally. You always align yourself with the wellspring of benefits.

You emotionally submit your burdens to God. We prayed, but nothing seemed to help. Life's burdens were becoming heavier by the day. I recall losing hope along the way. I stopped asking friends for support because we had done it before and received no help. We could hide our sorrows, hoping for a brighter tomorrow. My studio's business was at its lowest point since the COVID-19 outbreak. I considered starting another business, which reignited my desire to be a humanitarian.

In September 2023, Ambassador Dominic Obadiah phones to notify me that he is on a mentorship trip at a nearby school through the Top Talent Agency. I hurriedly joined him, along with my wife and son. Dr. M Teresa Lawrence appeared onstage. I remember she was giving a story about how they got past family issues as Cuban immigrants. I was moved by that outstanding testimony. We spoke after the event, and she gave me her two books, The Gloriousness and The Power of Leadership. The next day, we visited another school in my village. I sat next to her on the bus. She showed me photos of different places she had been. She enquired about my vision. I did not realize the divine contact that was extending his hands towards me. The day before, I moaned about my slow progress in life. I had reached the point of hopelessness. Thank God, everything happens for a purpose.

I was not able to complete the trip with them. My son's birthday was approaching soon. I needed to be present for his first birthday to bond with him. Dr. Teresa offered me $100, which truly helped me arrange almost everything for my son. After returning to the United States, I received an invitation to perform at the Fire Up live event from Marie Waite. I could not make it to the event, so I had to attend it virtually. I sang, and I received a certificate of honor. That was a turning point in my life and career. It energized my spirit. It sowed a new seed in my imagination. The seed of self-belief. I left a poisonous environment of differing viewpoints. Never let other people's opinions influence your mind. Once they have infiltrated your spirit and subconscious mind, it will need significant sacrifice to remove them. Do not buy opinions.

Lessons learnt

No one can readily achieve full success unless he rebukes and burns the bridges of delay. Always surround oneself with individuals of goodwill and willpower. I am now a renowned music producer. Am showing gratitude to everyone who has touched my life. I promise to reach out to many more with a blessed touch.

Pattie Godfrey~Sadler

THE MERAKI OF YOU

How many men or women do you know who have endured a lifelong use of methamphetamine and domestic abuse and lived to tell it? 95% of all families in the USA are affected by addiction, whether it be by the drug abuse itself or that of a family member. Drug abuse does not just affect the user; it compounds its ugly head upon anyone close to the addict. It causes dysfunctions in the family structure stemming to divorce, domestic abuse, elderly abuse, child abuse, and suicide.

About 38 years ago, I met a man. I was young and had not had any experience in the dating world. He was charming and interested in me and took me out to breakfast for a couple of weeks. I had been raised in a very religious home and he had as well so I figured it was safe although he had chosen not to go that route. A regular bad boy, I found it flattering that he noticed me and after a little time, he had me convinced that we were compatible. He was 8 years older than I was and so I believed he would know more about what to do in a relationship and that it would be secure. Everyone in the family advised me that I was moving too fast but that did not stop me from accepting a proposal.

We married quickly with a beautiful wedding. 250 guests and all of our families gathered. It was a beautiful wedding day. I was so excited to become a woman and a wife so I ignored all the signs that truly glared at me. Looking back, I am grateful for the son I received but so many lessons learned!

After we were married, we participated in drinking, smoking, and partying all the time. He approached me about using cocaine and I was really shocked. After a couple of times trying to convince me to "Join In", I reluctantly tried the poison. What I remember was the amazing feeling that I could do anything. He was a stickler about my weight so I also found this to be a way to keep very thin to be appealing to him.

The next part of our journey became a nightmare and I will not go into details here, but we ended up in a divorce.

Now that I was addicted to this drug, I began in the throes of my addiction. I met another man who I was immediately attracted to and we shared the addiction together. He was so handsome and so romantic that I thought it would last for forever.

After a year together, he started to show signs of abuse. The first time I felt it, he head bumped me for no reason. I was taken aback. I was not sure of what had just happened and I felt heartbroken for the first time. The abuse started to include subtleties of verbal abuse, accusations and just plain meanness. I was still in my early 20's and I decided that I would prove to him that I would do anything for him because I loved him so deeply. As I look back now, I was working for the devil.

As the abuse continued to increase with daily beatings and breaking down of morale, I would work harder by getting my journeyman license as a Carpenter and Iron Worker. I worked my body so hard and was in such incredible shape that I started to realize my own strength.

One day, I pushed back and he fell over. In that moment, I realized I had body strength that I had never experienced before. The result was me pushing back in every way. The abuse became two sided and continued for 17 years.

My drug addiction lasted 22 years. The abuse became unbearable. I had lost everything, including my children and I had had enough. I could not take it anymore. The self-sabotage, and self-destruction had taken its toll to a whole other level and everyone around me was suffering for my choices. I felt weak, unworthy, ugly, and the shame and guilt I felt were relentless. The abuse had left me feeling worthless and undesirable. I had to choose to love myself and live.

I made a choice. I had to live or die. I chose to live. I was blessed during that time to be found by my biological mother. That was a miracle in itself. When she found me, I had been incarcerated multiple times and was as thin as a rail. She gave me the opportunity to move to another state and start all over. I took it. I had nothing to lose and everything to gain. LIFE. I wanted to live. I wanted to pay penance for all that I had done and make a difference. Maybe some other woman was going through what I had been experiencing and if I could save just ONE, then thank the Lord.

I began my journey 16 years ago to reestablish my life and find meaning in my smallness. On the day that I arrived in my new chapter was the last day I ever used again.

I started with therapy, AA, NA, Church and reaching out to others who were living the life I wanted to lead. I left behind every last person and thing that would remind me of where I had been and I started all over with absolutely nothing. I had two beautiful children, and I would never be able to have them in my life if I did not choose me first. I chose ME and that changed my life forever.

The miracles that happened because of the one choice to live were astounding. I was married to a man whom I could trust, I was gainfully employed, I was also reunited with my children and have since become a grandmother and also became worthy to care for my elderly parents who passed in my care by falling asleep peacefully in their beds. I was blessed to make amends all the way around.

I want others to know that the decision to choose yourself over all others can be the most daunting choice a person can make. Especially when enveloped in domestic abuse, and codependency. Realizing that you are deserving of a life that contributes to the world is the first step to taking on your life. I did it. I know you can too.

Are you tired of living under the control of your past choices and other desires? The decision to choose to love yourself can give way to the discovery that we truly can create what we deeply desire in our hearts.

The Meraki of choosing your own worth and sharing your story will lead to a passionate journey. I wish to share with you the magic of choosing Oneself as a passion. That very choice can change the world. Literally.

Once we realize that we are miracles manifest and divinely destined for greatness, we can take on the truth of who we truly are. That is when we can decide to create success for ourselves, even in the smallest of ways.

Making a choice. Making The Choice. The one that suggests we are done not willing to sacrifice ourselves for those things and people that are destroying us. This is the only way that the Mighty Transformation can take place and our new journey will begin. Success lies just on the other side of it. It is within our reach as soon as we realize our worth.

Success is not really determined by the amount of money one has or the material gifts that have been acquired. Success is the actual ability to be impassioned about something specific and create an empire around that desire. Perhaps being passionate about loving oneself? Start there.

Once we have learned of our own worth, our own message might be the passion that drives us to heal others. Sharing our stories can light the way for healing on such a big level and the ripple effects are enormous. Give your lesson away and let it float like a butterfly to others so they can see that it is possible for them to be the miracles in their own lives. There are no boundaries unless we believe in them. There are no limitations unless we limit ourselves. With passion, desire, hard work, determination and one can create ANYTHING. However, you have to BELIEVE that you are divinely created for greatness first.

It does not cost money to make a difference. It takes passion, desire and kindness and with those attributes, anything is possible.

My dad used to speak at church as a leader and his sermons could be summed up in a little poem that he shared frequently.

> *"A bell's not a bell 'til you ring it, a song's not a song 'til you sing it, Love in your heart was not put there to stay, and Love isn't love 'til you give it away!"*
>
> *Oscar Hammerstein II*

Over the years, I have been fascinated with my own self-development and finding techniques to meditate, heal myself, and raise my frequency. I have built an empire and created entrepreneurship through a desire to share a story to invite others to realize their own worth. I would like to share six steps that I have incorporated in my life to give back what I have learned and find success in my own life. I hope that with these points, you will be motivated to find your way into this fascinating lifestyle of loving yourself enough to give to others.

The Miracle is YOU.

1. Find a passion, interest, a purpose, or talent that could lift others up. These could all be combined into one category. For instance, I have a passion for the human experience, I love to write, my cause is to uplift women globally to realize their potential and I have a talent for motivating others and making people smile. All qualities that I have are my very own and they are special to me. They build a foundation from that which I love. By finding the qualities that bring me joy and enable me to offer services and kindness to others, I have found a passion that I can build on. The passion that I have is to help others and create sunshine in their lives. What are your passions? What are your talents? Who can help you to develop those talents to your best ability?

2. Make use of your talents. Offer service where you are able. Be willing to give of your talents to others to lift them up. Find out that by doing so you are creating joy in your life. Learn that you can make a difference and that you can change lives. Using your talents will give you the confidence and ability to create that which you desire. By sharing what you have you will come to believe in yourself and realize that what you have to offer is of great worth.

3. Get Clarity in all areas of your life. Your life is complete by five areas that need to be balanced. Consider your health, your spirituality, your personal development, your personal relationships and your financial and career development. These five areas need to be balanced in a way that you are clear in the very direction you wish to go. Some get personal coaching, some use journaling and writing to express their plan, while others find information online and gather it up to create their success. Find programs that will give you the personal development or coaching you need to create this vision to happen. There are many resources available these days to help you put everything together, meditate, and get clarity on your plan of action. Once you have that clarity, you can create an empire beyond your own limitations.

4. Your mind believes what it is told. Take time to meditate daily, create on paper how you would like to see your life turn out, what you would like to improve on and goals you would like to achieve. Feed yourself with positive influence all around you. Avoid negative thoughts and actions and change your responses to be that of a positive nature. Write down the things you want to create as if you have already created them and read them daily. Ponder and pray over these things you wish to create, and you will find inspiration all around you.

5. Envision your dream and own it. Once you have put into practice your talents, giving back to others and gaining the confidence, being clear with all five categories in your life, take that clarity and take on your life. If you are good at something, make it yours and BRAND it. Go and create business cards to affirm that which you are creating. Start putting things in motion, as that is who you are becoming.

If you are starting a business to consult others, create a business card that states that you are a consultant and what your specialty of consultation is. If you are beginning a project in form of a gift to the world, state your talent in form of a title and own that title. Share with others your excitement for that which you are creating and motivate others to get involved. Believe in yourself and take it on. You are the only one who can own this creative effort. Once an entrepreneur, always one and to become one means you are already creative.

6. Make it happen. Share your ideas, network with theirs, and create a LinkedIn account and other forms of social media to connect with others doing the same. Choose your associations wisely and associate with the kinds of people you wish to be like. Advertise your services and make it known what you are doing. Remember that your talent and ability to help others is worth something and charge for your services. There are many ways to claim an income doing what you love. People are hungry to become more and develop in their life. They are hungry for your services and in need of your services.

Believe in yourself, contact and get the word out and you may be surprised at what you have already done.

Lastly, I would like to invite you to consider an idea that has given me the opportunity to brand myself in ways I never imagined. Remember that money is not the motivator. Giving to the world and creating gifts and doing what you love is.

Following your dreams and passions should be the goal. The bonus is the money we create. It allows us to contribute to society, sustain and provide for our families and offer better quality of life, not only for ourselves but also for all who come into our circle.

I believe that playing small does not serve anyone and least of all ourselves. We were created to create.

We were meant to make a difference in this world and find joy in serving others.

We were also endowed with responsibilities to contribute our talents and provide for our earthly needs.

There is no reason why you should not believe that you are able to create anything your heart desires.

So be fierce, entrepreneur warriors. Become your own miracle and change the world!

www.ingramcontent.com/pod-product-compliance
Lightning Source LLC
LaVergne TN
LVHW012026060526
838201LV00061B/4478